A Reason For Being

THE PHILOSOPHY
OF MONODEITISM

BY
S. BRADFORD WILLIAMS, JR.

THE COPPER ORCHID PUBLISHING COMPANY
JACKSON, MICHIGAN

I dedicate
that which is written within

To my God
and
To all of Mankind

Artwork by: JoAnne Holbrook
Illustrations designed by: S. Bradford Williams Jr.
Other books by the Author: Caress Softly Thy Love
Sunshine Grows The Day

Published by:
THE COPPER ORCHID PUBLISHING COMPANY
1966 Westbrook Dr.
Jackson, Michigan 49201

THE COPPER ORCHID PUBLISHING COMPANY

Printed in the United States of America
First printing—August 1984

ISBN: 0-9608522-2-0
Library of Congress Catalog Card Number: 84-71446

A Reason For Being

Introduction

This, the Philosophy of Monodeitism, hasn't been written for everyone. It couldn't be. For all of us are at different levels of understanding; in various stages of development; on separate and unique planes of evolvement. Monodeitism, or the Doctrines of One God ("mono" meaning "one"; "deity" meaning "God"; "ism" meaning "doctrines of"), examines the intent behind life and existence, and, as such, is the purpose for the writing of *A Reason For Being*.

This book couldn't be written for everyone—just for those individuals who've begun to awaken, or have awakened to the reality of what they are, and how this reality relates to that which surrounds them.

Some will find the book offensive; a threat to their ideals, their life-concepts and, ultimately, to their beliefs.

Others will find the book enlightening; an inspiration which fosters knowledge, stirs thought and challenges the imagination.

Still in all, it's essential to remember that all that's found within, is truth as perceived by the author. The book is not designed to injure any individual's sense of well-being, but, inherent in the nature of what has been written, it probably shall. For this is the way of change; the way by which we learn and mature. Sometimes growth is a painful and stressful experience; sometimes it is effortless and pleasant.

Remember, too, that *A Reason For Being* has been created to do good; not harm. And, as such, the following is offered as a partial justification for any distress that may be caused.

> If the book moves you and instills contentment; then it is good. If it disturbs you and effects new and creative thought; then it is good. If it makes you angry and inspires the defense and reaffirmation of already held beliefs; then it is good. No matter how one construes the philosophy detailed within—no matter how one interprets or feels about the book's doctrines and beliefs—*it is constructive and it is good.*

S. Bradford Williams Jr.
June of 1984

Part One

The Concept of God

All life that surrounds us
is God.
    All nonlife that surrounds us
    is God.
        Both the finite and the infinite
        are God.

So be not afraid.
For you too are of God
    existing within
        the completeness of His totality.

Before it's possible to contemplate the "whys" of existence, we must first establish a fundamental, foundation of ideals from which to communicate ideas and thoughts. In order to accomplish this, let us think back to our days of "basic geometry" and remember, that in its language, it uses the term "axiom".

An axiom is: "a proposition regarded as a self-evident truth".[1]

Thus, it could be said, that an axiom is a fact that need not be proven, because it's so obviously true, it's not necessary to do so. All philosophical doctrines are based upon axioms. And, whereas geometry is formulated upon "self-evident mathematical truths", a religious or philosophical doctrine is formulated upon "self-evident philosophical truths". The problem with self-evident philosophical truths, as well as with self-evident mathematical truths, is in the "who" that's doing the defining. Certainly, not all philosophies hold to, or are formulated upon, the same self-evident philosophical truths. For if they were, all theologies and philosophies would be alike. The same is true with geometry. There is Euclidean and Non-Euclidean Geometry, which are actually two different mathematical viewpoints, each of which is based upon two different sets of obvious, "self-evident mathematical truths". In other words, someone, at some time, perceived that Euclid had not seen the whole truth. This insight, in turn, caused the creation of an entirely new type of geometry, which became known as Non-Euclidean Geometry.

So, where does this leave us? It leaves us with this fact — any and all truths are of the individual. Therefore, should an individual elect to accept and internalize another person's truths, he or she must believe that these truths are real.

Detailed below, and yours to either accept or reject, are the fifteen primary truths — the fifteen foundation axioms upon which this philosophy is based. They are, for all intents and purposes — *The Fundamentals Of Existence.*

The Fifteen Foundation Axioms

of the

Philosophy of Monodeitism

1. There is God. A something greater than the self.
2. God is the Whole; a perfect, totalness complete.
3. There is I. I do exist; separate, but a part of the Whole.
4. There is nonlife; the nonliving substances that surround all life.
5. There is life; the me. Each living entity's mortal force.
6. There is soul; the I am. Each living entity's immortal force.
7. All nonlife is a part of God; a part of the Whole.
8. All life is a part of God; a part of the Whole.
9. All soul is a part of God; a part of the Whole.
10. Nonlife is static. It does not grow, mature and develop.
11. Life, which possesses total aliveness, is not static. It must grow, mature and develop.
12. Soul is not static. It must grow, mature and develop.
13. Nonlife has no soul.
14. Life has no soul, unless it possesses total aliveness.
15. Soul exists without life.

The above fifteen axioms are logical and ordered. Existence, too, is logical and ordered. Each one of the above listed maxims is absolutely essential to the formulation of a totally, unified philosophy. For these are the fundamentals of existence; the very basis for our being able to understand—our reason for being.

There are always those who are skeptical about the existence of God, and whether or not He takes an active role in guiding and controlling that which He has created. The following analysis should alleviate any such doubts and/or skepticisms.

During each and every moment of living, all of us are confronted with having to make choices and decisions about which pathways—life courses—we are going to take. Each decision is affected by known and unknown influences. Each decision creates known and unknown consequences.

To put this concept into other words—in living, each of us is faced with an infinite number of possible pathways that require us to make choices and decisions. These choices and decisions are always *caused* by, and because of, something and are always *effected* by, and because of, something. It's these "somethings" that are either known or unknown.

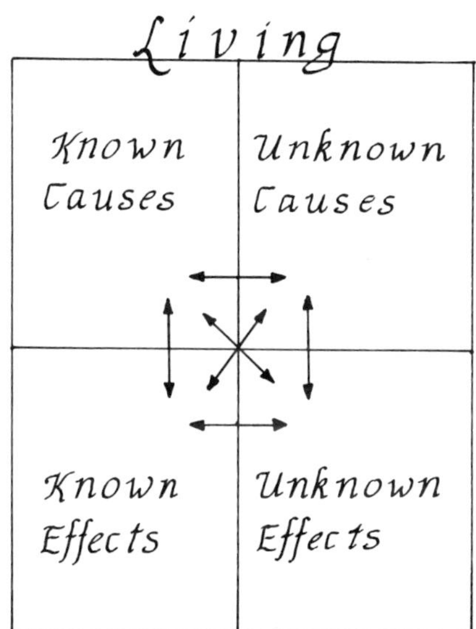

Living, then, is having to decide and choose which way to go, while knowing that each choice or decision is influenced by known and unknown causes and effects. It's in the areas that remain "unknown" to us that we, inevitably, become aware of God's presence. For, it's in these areas, where it becomes apparent, that the "hand of God" is involved in existence. The following examples will help illustrate the above concept.

Example number 1 –

A man is faced with having to decide, whether or not he will accept a new and different job in another city.

Known causes:

The known causes that brought him to this crossroad in life were: the need for a change in surroundings; the need for more money; the need for new friends; and so forth.

Unknown causes:

The unknown causes are those things that are making the man want to move: the "what" that's behind the need for a change in atmosphere; the "why" that's behind the need for more money; the "what" and the "why" that's behind the need for new friends. Some of these "what" and "why" questions are answerable. Yet, if one relentlessly queries the man's reasons for moving with questions like: "What's making you do this?"; or, "Why are you doing that?"; he'll eventually arrive at a point in time where he'll have to say: "I don't know why."; and, he really won't know. It's when he finally arrives at this point, that he'll have reached that moment when known causes end and unknown causes begin.

******

The man decides to accept the job and moves to the other city. By accepting the job and moving to the other city, his decision creates, for himself and others, known and unknown effects.

Known effects:

Some of the known effects, created by his decision are: having to locate a new doctor and dentist; having to find a new house; having to place his children in a new school system.

Unknown effects:

The unknown effects, on the other hand, are those things that he can't foresee influencing him, until after he encounters them. Things such as: "how" the new people surrounding him will adjust to his presence; "how" the dentist and the doctor will accept him as a patient; "how" the realtor will assist him as a customer.

******

Each known cause creates the need to make new choices and decisions. When the man finally comes into contact with the other people (ie. the doctor, the dentist, his fellow employees), he becomes a known cause, creating in them, the need to make new choices and decisions. Their decisions and choices will be based upon past causes and effects. In other words, the doctor and dentist will have to decide and choose, whether or not they will accept the man as a patient, based upon their present needs and past prejudices. The same is true with the people he'll be working with, and with the realtor who will be selling him his house. Each act—each decision and choice that he makes, binds him to that act and its consequences, making him act and then act again. This is also true for the others he comes into contact with.

Living

Known Causes	Unknown Causes
1. The need for a change. 2. The need for more money. 3. The need for new friends. 4. Etc.	1. The ultimate reason "why" a change is needed. 2. The ultimate reason "why" more money is needed. 3. The ultimate reason "why" new friends are needed. 4. "Why" and "what" are the ultimate causes behind the need to move. 5. Etc.
Known Effects	**Unknown Effects**
1. Having to locate a new doctor and dentist. 2. Having to find a new house. 3 Having to place the man's children in a new school system. 4. Etc.	1 "How" will the new doctor or dentist accept the man. 2. "How" will the realtor assist the man in finding a new home. 3. "How" will the man's children be accepted by their new classmates. 4. "What" are the far reaching effects of the man's moving. "Whom" will they effect and "how". 5. Etc.

Example number 2–

For the moment, if you think back to the time when you were in high school, learning about nuclear energy, you may remember that a chain reaction was demonstrated by filling a small room with ping pong balls, placed upon ready-to-spring mouse traps. When all was ready, someone threw a ping pong ball into the middle of the room. Before long, ping pong balls were flying everywhere; with one ping pong ball setting off another ping pong ball which, in turn, set off other ping pong balls, and so forth, until eventually, most of the traps were sprung and spent ping pong balls were scattered all over the floor.

If we equate a single ping pong ball to that of one man, we can then visualize how a person—a single entity—(the ping pong ball that's thrown into the middle of the room), through his choices and decisions, can influence an entire community of men (the ping pong balls resting on the ready-to-spring traps) into reacting with each other.

Known cause:

The known cause, in the total reaction, is the first ping pong ball dropping onto the ready-to-spring trap of the second ping pong ball. In other words, the first ping pong ball starts everything by dropping onto the second ping pong ball. The second ping pong ball "knows" what's making it react. It "knows" that the first ping pong ball fell onto its trap pan. So, the second ping pong ball reacts, and, with the first ping pong ball, flies off into the air to influence and induce other ping pong balls into doing the same.

As we get further and further into the chain reaction—as we get further and further away from the collision of the first and second ping pong balls—we will find that the ping pong balls in the later part of the reaction process, are "unaware" of the entire chain of events. They are only "aware" of the most immediate ping pong ball that fell directly upon them, or perhaps, the activated ping pong ball before that one.

This, then, creates what appears to be unknown causes inducing reaction, but which, in reality, can still be traced back to the very first ping pong ball. So, even though all of the parts are not "aware" of everything, and of every influence, the entire chain reaction can be traced back to its known cause—that of the first ping pong ball falling upon the trap of the second ping pong ball.

Unknown cause:

The unknown cause is the "why" the first ping pong ball was thrown into the room, as well as the "what" and the "who" that had tossed it. In other words, all of the ping pong balls are sitting quietly upon their ready-to-spring traps when, from out of nowhere, a single ping pong ball drops into the middle of the room and creates total chaos. None of the ping pong balls in the room know "what", "why" or "who" tossed the first ping pong ball in amongst them. This is the unknown cause, and in this example, is the equivalent of the "hand of God" influencing and controlling existence.

Known effect:

The known effect, on the other hand, is the fact that the second ping pong ball sprang into the air when the first ping pong ball hit its ready-to-spring trap. Because it reacted, and it does, indeed, fly into the air, its reaction is a known effect.

Unknown effect:

The unknown effect is something that happens because of an unknown cause. Let's say that a ping pong ball, "A", has had another ping pong ball drop upon its trap. Ping pong ball "A" "decides" and "chooses" to

Living

Known Cause	Unknown Cause
The second ping pong ball "knows" the first ping pong ball is causing it to react; The known cause.	The first ping pong ball does not "know" "why", "what" or "who" threw it into the room full of ping pong balls sitting on ready-to-spring traps; the unknown cause.
Known Effect	**Unknown Effect**
The second ping pong ball flies into the air to react with other ping pong balls. It "knows" it is reacting; The known effect.	Ping pong balls "A" and "B", for "no apparent reason", are blown off course, collide with each other and strike two unsuspecting ping pong balls. Until they strike the two unsuspecting ping pong balls, the effect is unknown

fly to the right, because it wants to "influence" a friend on the other side of the room. In the meantime, ping pong ball "B" has also been struck and is reacting. It, in turn, has "decided" and "chosen" to fly to the left, because it, too, wants to "influence" one of its friends. Everything is going as planned, however, while in midair, and as they are speeding toward their intended goals, a strong breeze comes up (over which they have no control) and causes them to veer into each other. Instead of flying to the right, to reach its intended goal, ping pong ball "A" ends up hitting the trap of some unsuspecting ping pong ball for "no apparent reason". The same is true for ping pong ball "B". The unknown effect, then, is the reaction which has been created by the unknown cause. The unknown cause is the "why" and the "who" that sent the inopportune wind at that particular instant in time. The unknown effect remains unknown until ping pong balls "A" and "B" realize they aren't going towards their "chosen" goals, and, "for no apparent reason", are falling upon someone else. It's the unknown effect that creates, in each of us, those feelings of: "Why, me?".

Example number 3 –

A husband and wife were going to fly to Florida for their vacation. Before their vacation could take place, the husband fell down and broke his leg. He was in the hospital at the time the plane left for Florida. Both the husband and wife were very disappointed about not being able to go to Florida, until they later learned that the plane had crashed, killing all persons aboard.

******

It's when we come to acknowledge and accept the existence of unknown causes and effects, realizing we are sometimes involved in situations not of our choosing, and over which we have no control, that we also become cognizant of the "hand of God" manipulating and controlling existence. God's control becomes the most evident, when we come to realize that we are being prodded by unknown causes and effects. We have named these unknown and uncontrollable influences: luck, joss, happenstance, karma, fate, fortune, chance and so forth.

It's hard to understand and fathom why there are people who do not believe in the existence of God, especially when there are so many examples of where "fate has intervened" – where the "hand of God" has influenced an individual's destiny.

Fate, luck, fortune and the like are the indicators – the visible signs that point to a very active God. A God, who demonstrates His existence through unknown causes and unknown effects. A God, who is maintaining an ordered existence.

As one observes and studies mankind of today, it can be seen that there is a new consciousness burgeoning, and, inherent as a part of this internal awakening, is an irresistible need to know the "real" God. It's this all-encompassing need that creates, within us, an insight into "what" God must be. Linked with this insight, is the realization that what we have been, and are still being, taught by the religions of today, is, in part, a travesty and a contradiction to the truth of God.

This observation can best be explained and illustrated, by using several quotations which have been extracted from the Old and New Testaments of the Bible.

> "Therefore wait ye upon me saith the Lord, . . . that I may assemble the kingdoms, to pour upon them mine indignation, even all my fierce anger: for all the earth shall be devoured with the fire of my jealousy." (Zep. 3:8)[2]
>
> "So will I send upon you famine and evil beasts, and they shall bereave thee; and pestilence and blood shall pass through thee; and I will bring the sword upon thee. I the Lord have spoken it." (Eze. 5:17)[3]
>
> "And the Lord said unto Moses . . . Now therefore let me alone, that my wrath may wax hot against them, and that I may consume them; . . . And the Lord repented of the evil which he thought to do unto his people." (Exo. 32:9; 32:10; 32:14)[4]
>
> "And we have known and believed the love that God hath to us. God is love; and he that dwelleth in love dwelleth in God, and God in him." (I John 4:16)[5]
>
> ". . . Be perfect, be of good comfort, be of one mind, live in peace; and the God of love and peace shall be with you." (II Cor. 13:11)[6]
>
> "And the Lord passed by before Him, and proclaimed, the Lord, the Lord God, merciful and gracious, longsuffering, and abundant in goodness and truth, Keeping mercy for thousands, forgiving iniquity and transgression and sin, . . ." (Exo. 34:6; 34:7)[7]

Note that the first three quotations, define God as being a wrathful, vengeful and evil entity. The last three quotations define Him as being a loving, protective and all-understanding creator. Therein lies the contradiction in ideals. How can God be both good and bad? How can He be both perfect, and yet, flawed with evil? The answer, of course, is that he cannot.

Mankind has, in the course of time, come to realize that today's religious teachings, and not just those of Judiasm and Christianity, are filled with ambiguities in believability and logic. Such a realization causes a tremendous, inner turmoil—a turmoil that has been created by needing to accept, on faith, what one's religion is teaching, yet, at the same time, knowing that it is illogical and incorrect. As a consequence, a desire to know and understand the "real" God builds up within, causing that same individual to turn away from his or her childhood religion.

The Philosophy of Monodeitism is different from today's religions, in that it holds to two main ideals which are essential to its fundamental, foundation of beliefs. They are: *God exists;* and, *God is absolute (total) perfection.* These are the first two foundation axioms—the first two of its fifteen primary laws of existence. With absolute certainty, it can be stated that the majority of us believe in, and accept, these two axioms, even though contemporary religions are not teaching them as ultimate truths. For God is perfect and perfection implies, by definition, that the thing or entity so described, has to possess: "Qualities, traits and features of the highest excellence".[8] A "God" who finds a need to create and instill fear, distress and pain—who is capable of being wrathful, vengeful and evil in his dealings with creatures who are weak and fragile—is an imperfect being. The Christian God, as defined by the Bible, is imperfect. For how can one construe vengeance, wrath and evilness as being traits and features of the "highest excellence," when they are, so obviously, exactly the opposite? God is not evil, nor is God imperfect. So then, "what" is God?

Monodeitism defines God as being love. God is also peace and wisdom and truth. God is good and pure and protective. God is all-forgiving, all-comforting, all-giving, all-merciful and all-understanding. God is any and all of those descriptive adjectives we use to define goodness in existence.

The above defines "what" God is, but it does not address the question of "who" He is. In many of the religions of today, God is described and portrayed as a separate, all-powerful entity who sits in Heaven, passing judgments on mankind during life and after death. This description elicits an image of a very remote and dispassionate God. It exemplifies, again, an entity of imperfection—an entity who, because he remains separate, lacks completeness.

Monodeitism, on the other hand, defines God as you and I. God is our body and soul. God is also the grass, the stars, the planets, the Earth, the rocks, the seas, the birds, and the flowers. God is everything—both the living and the non-living; both the void and the non-void. God is the Whole.

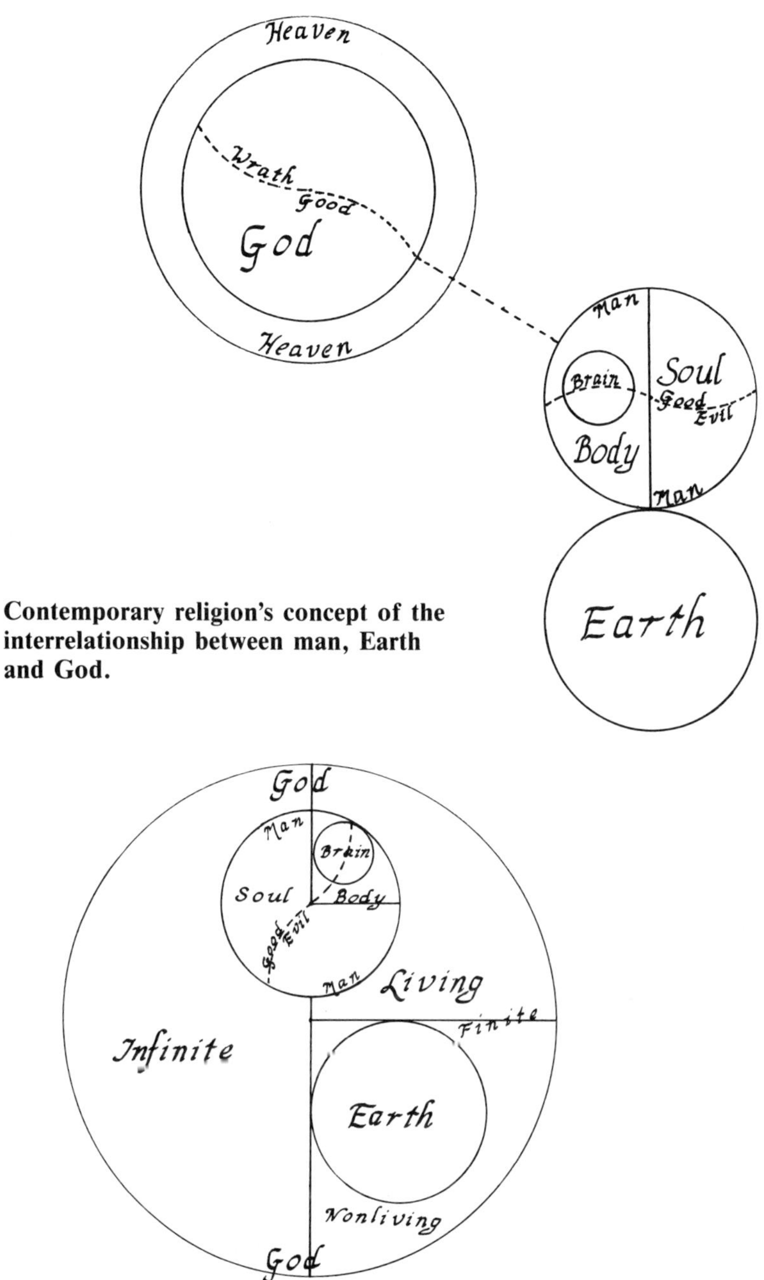

Contemporary religion's concept of the interrelationship between man, Earth and God.

Monodeitism's concept of the interrelationship between man, Earth and God.

The following analogy will help illustrate Monodeitism's conceptualization of "who" God is and "how" mankind fits into His totality.

First, let us liken God unto a tree. God is the trunk, the limbs, the roots and the leaves. God is all of the tree's many parts. He is all of its parts and, too, all of its parts are He.

Second, let us liken mankind unto the leaves, so that each leaf represents a single man. Each leaf, as with each man, is independent and has a life of its own—a life that has the freedom to sway as it will with the breeze, while, at the same time, remaining a necessary, included part of the whole. Each leaf, as with each man, draws its sustenance from the whole and, also, gives its sustenance back to nurture the total. Even in death, when the leaf falls from the tree to decay at the base of the trunk, it continues to give of its existence to nourish the entirety.

All of this leads us to a very, interesting question. Specifically—how can a something that is totally perfect, also have as a part of it, a something that is imperfect? In other words, how can God be totally perfect, when mankind, as a part of God's totality, exhibits "traits, qualities and features that are *not* of the highest excellence"? And, since man's character constantly manifests traits, qualities and features that are less than perfect—traits such as: creating and causing fear, inflicting wrath and/or dealing in vengeance—does not man's imperfection, also mean, that God is imperfect?

The answer is "no". God is a perfect, totalness complete and man is a perfect part of God's totalness.

The terms "perfection" and "imperfection", it must be noted, presume, by definintion, that there has been an ending—a finality—that the something, which the words refer to, is the epitome of what it can be. God is such a finality, but mankind is still evolving. Man has yet to become the epitome of what he can become. He is still growing. Therefore, because man has not reached his finality; because he continues to evolve; he, also, hasn't arrived at a point where he can be deemed to be perfect or imperfect. He is, instead, still *noncomplete.* Noncomplete, then, describes an entity (or a something) who is still in the throes of evolvement.

God is a warm, gentle and loving Creator. He is no more, and no less, complicated than what has been described and defined. Mankind, as a part of God, is also of His perfection. Because we be a part of God, we be of His perfection—a *noncomplete* part of the perfect Whole.

Once we acknowledge the actually of unknown causes and unknown effects, we are also, then, forced to accept the fact that God, in His active role, is using these elements to control that which He has created. But, does God maintain total control, over all things, at all times?

The answer to this question is a qualified "no". The reason it's a qualified "no" is, that for us, mankind, God's control is not total. We have the ability to choose. We, you and I, being the most advanced of all life forms on Earth, are granted the greatest ability to make choices and decisions about which life course(s) we are going to take. We are also accorded the greatest ability for understanding "why" we took a specific pathway; a pathway that may even be contrary to the "will of God".

To be able to choose and decide implies, by definition, that an entity has the ability to know and understand the reason(s) behind a specific choice or decision. This ability varies from entity to entity—from a high ability of knowing and understanding "why", to a complete inability to even make a choice or decision.

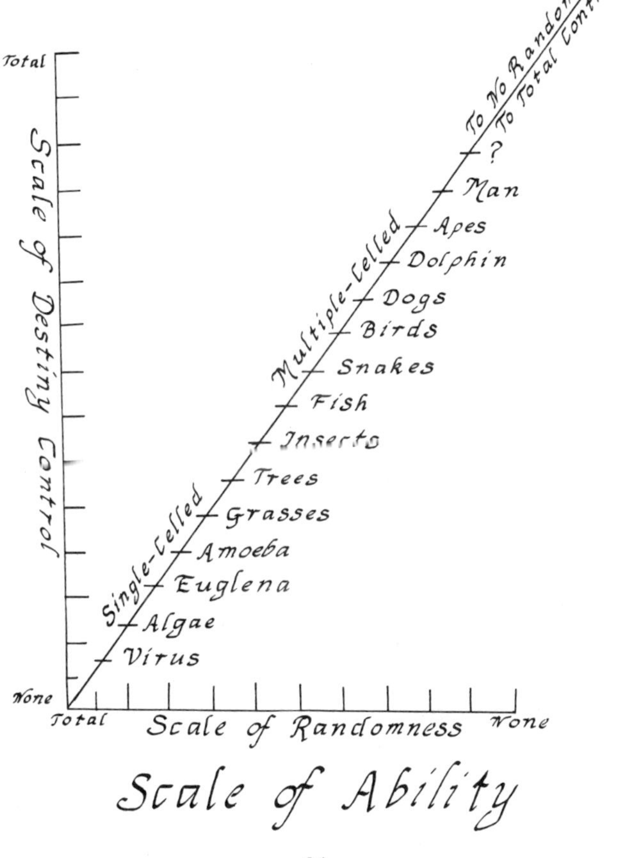

Scale of Ability

Every entity has the right—the freedom to choose and decide which life course(s) it desires to take. However, not every entity has the ability to do so. Because of this fact, we are inevitably led to the conclusion that existence in the lower orders of life must, due to an entity's lack of ability, be random actions—that randomness and ability are directly related to where an entity is located within the various levels of life.

Thus, the higher an entity is in the order of life, the more ability it possesses to know and understand "why" it makes a choice or decision, and the less random, more calculated its acts become. And vice versa. The lower an entity is in the order of life, the less ability it possesses to know and understand "why" it does what it does, and the more random, less calculated its acts become. To put this another way; the higher the entity is in the order of life, the more it controls its own destiny.

No entity we know of, has reached the point where it possesses the total ability to know and understand "why" it chooses as it does. Nor has any entity gained total control over its destiny; a fact that has been thoroughly discussed, and illustrated, in the section dealing with known and unknown causes and effects. It should also be noted, that based upon the *Scale of Ability,* it appears as if life is evolving toward a moment in existence when there will be an entity, who has total awareness and complete destiny control. Because the *Scale of Ability* leads us to this conclusion, one can only wonder if this isn't that point in time when the finite finally attains the state of *near-perfection; near-perfection* because the finite can *never* achieve *total perfection.*

The *Scale of Ability* illustrates that there is growth and change in existence which means, that during life, living is neither foreordained, nor predestined. It also means that God allows us, as human beings, to have the most control and freedom over our own lives. We are accorded the greatest ability to make choices and decisions, and although our abilities do not include total control, God's control over us is not total either. We can, and often do, make decisions and choices that are contrary to the "will of God". We can, and often do, choose a life course that is against correctness in existence. We can, and sometimes do, choose a pathway that is totally wrong in nature. Yet, even though we are, on an individual basis, allowed to choose a life course that is contrary to "God's will", God does not allow mankind's existence to run rampant. Man, as a whole, has not been given total freedom. God keeps and maintains His control over all existence, which varies, depending upon how advanced a specific entity is in life. Mankind is at that point in evolution, and on the *Scale of Ability,* where, he wouldn't be able to cope with total freedom. He'd, more than likely, destroy himself as a species. So, mankind has not been, nor will he be, given the opportunity to totally annihilate or eliminate himself as part of God's existence—*even though he believes he can.*

Ponder, for a moment, what has just been stated. Unknown causes and effects, known causes and effects, the *Scale of Ability,* randomness versus nonrandomness; all of these factors, when combined, demonstrate and illustrate, that although we, mankind as a whole, may think we are in *complete control*; even though we may believe that we have *total control* over the direction in which we are going to progress—*we do not*. God has the final say about how existence is going to develop. God, by way of His unknown causes and effects, is constantly creating change, which, in turn, also creates, especially for mankind, the necessity of compensating for the same.

Which brings us back to the topic of predestination; a very important concept and one that should be made as clear as possible. It's important to realize that there *is* predestination, and, there *is not* predestination; which sounds contradictory, but really isn't. If we were to draw a time-line continuum from the beginning of time to the present, we would see that there is a definite route—a course of existence—that is being taken; a route that is leading, for the infinite, to total perfection, and, for the finite, to near-perfection. In this respect, as far as the overall "master plan" is concerned, the course of existence is predestined.

On the other hand, if we were to take a small segment out of this time-line continuum, and enlarge it so that we could look at one person's life, from birth to death, we would see, that even though this individual is of the predestined "master plan", his life is not foreordained. It's not foreordained because he has the freedom—the right—to choose which life course(s) he is going to take. It is "the right of choice" which leads us to the conclusion that life, on an individual basis, *is not* predestined.

Inherent, too, as an integral part of this conclusion, is the realization that we are also allowed to do anything, during life, we want or wish to do. However, if we elect to follow a life course which is wrong in its nature, we shall suffer the painful consequences of our having made an incorrect decision. So, how do we go about making the correct decision?

God provides us with assistance in choosing a proper life course. He provides us with guidance; an internal and external guidance system, so to speak. It's a system recognized and known as the "inner voice"—conscience, if you will—as well as a sense, or a feeling, of the rightness or wrongness of one's actions.

We have the freedom to heed or ignore the "inner voice" and, too, there are times when we misread which direction the "inner voice" wishes us to take. There are also those times, when we don't feel as though we are being guided, but we are. God's guidance is constant and ongoing. All that's necessary is that we "listen".

Yet, God's guidance is more than just an "internal voice"; more than just a sense of the rightness or wrongness of one's actions. It's both of these factors, coupled with positive or negative external happenings, which denote/allude to the correctness or incorrectness of one's acts.

In other words, if a proper pathway has been chosen—if the "inner voice" has been listened to and heeded—one will know that a correct life course has been taken, not only because it will feel right, but also, because those activities needed to complete the act, will all come out right. This process, that of knowing things are correct, is being called *cognitive reassurances.*

However, should an incorrect life course be chosen— should the "inner voice" have been ignored and/or misinterpreted—one will know that a wrong pathway has been taken, not only because it will feel wrong, but also, because those activities needed to complete the act, will all come out wrong. This process, that of knowing things are not correct, is being called *cognitive impedances.*

It's important to recognize that we are accorded the freedom and the ability to choose our life courses; that we are accorded the freedom and ability to accept or reject God's guidance—this includes paying heed to our conscience, paying heed to cognitive impedances and/or paying heed to cognitive reassurances; that we are accorded the freedom and ability to make our own choices and decisions, *but,* that we are still, as individuals, responsible for our actions. We are responsible for the *pursuit of correctness in existence.* One indication that correctness in existence is being pursued, is from cognitive reassurances.

Likewise, if we elect to ignore or reject God's guidance, we will have to pay the consequences for our actions. These consequences are imposed upon us by way of cognitive impedances. Our life will go so far awry, be filled with such unhappiness, that we will, usually, do anything to make it better. It's the discontentment; the depression; the bad luck; that creates, in us, the need to seek the life course that God wanted us to take in the first place. *But, we don't have to.*

It's also important to realize, that we don't always know "who" or "what" we may be influenceing. It's our responsibility to make sure, as much as we are capable, that the acts we commit produce good and that correctness in existence is being pursued. We, as mankind, are required to use our ability to reason, and our freedom, with prudence and forethought. We are charged with the responsibility of, in all things, acting wisely and for the good of all existence.

A major inconsistency, or contradiction, appears to have arisen out of what has, thus far, been written. Specifically—how can it be concluded, that God is not, at times, a "God of love", and, at other times, a "God of wrath"? Is it not obvious that the "hand of God" moves through existence in the form of luck or fate, and, that there are many instances when this luck or fate is bad and hurtful? Doesn't this fact point to a God of ambivalence—one, who creates both the good and the bad—one, who is *both* benevolent and malevolent?

The answer is: "No, it does not". There are no contradictions or inconsistencies in God. God is a perfect, totalness complete.

Even though we can and do see the "hand of God" manipulating existence by unknown causes and unknown effects; and even though it appears as if we have no control over these happenings; it must be remembered that these happenings, ill-fated or otherwise, are occurring because of a life course we had chosen. Since we are accorded the most freedom and ability to decide "what" we are going to do, and "how" we are going to do it, we are, for the most part, the creators of our own luck. In other words, we reap what we sow.

As to the other part of the question—that of a "God of two faces"—it must be remembered that the portrayal of this kind of God has been a part of our heritage for many, many centuries. In fact, the belief that God is both good, and sometimes, justly wrathful, is a concept which is still being taught by the major religions of today. Their doctrines, of the "scheme of things", can be described as including: man, who is both good and bad; God, who is both benevolent and justly malevolent; and Satan, who is evil. If we were to create a basic, graphic representation of this conceptualization, it would look like this.

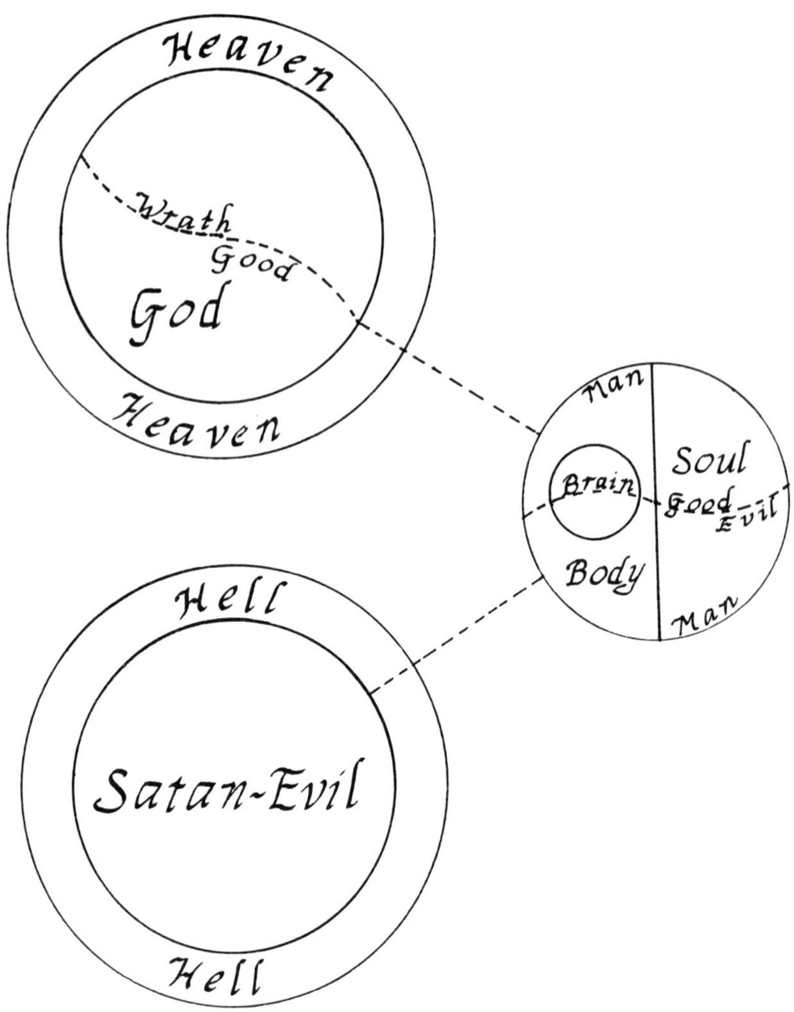

Contemporary religion's basic viewpoint of how God, Satan and man fit into the "scheme of things".

Because the Philosophy of Monodeitism believes there is no inconsistency in God (that malevolence, even "just" malevolence, is that of "wishing evil to another or others"[9] — a contradiction to God's perfection — and, that God is, in all things, good and benevolent) then, it must be concluded that the traits of good and evil are found only in those entities, such as mankind, who are noncomplete. Below are several illustrations of the Monodeitistic conceptualization of God's totality, and "how" man, animal, plant, good and evil, and so forth all fit within His perfection.

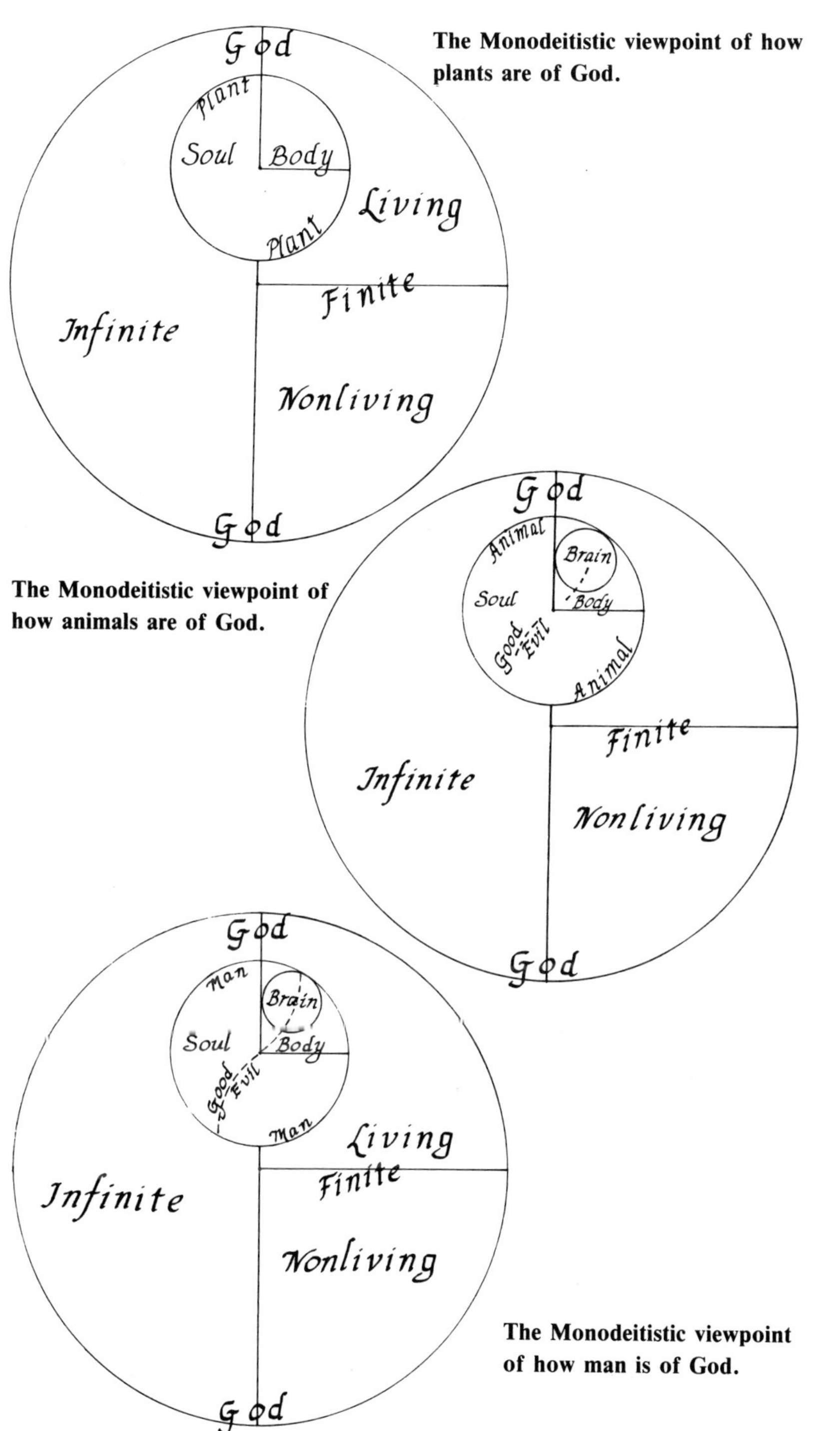

The Monodeitistic viewpoint of how plants are of God.

The Monodeitistic viewpoint of how animals are of God.

The Monodeitistic viewpoint of how man is of God.

Continuing along these same lines of logic, it can also be illustrated "how" the religions of Christianity and Judaism have created a very, complicated set of beliefs in order to incorporate all of the essential parts needed to support their philosophical doctrines. These essential parts include (besides God, Satan and man) such things as: the Virgin Mary, angels, demons, Hell, Heaven, the Holy Spirit and Jesus the Christ.

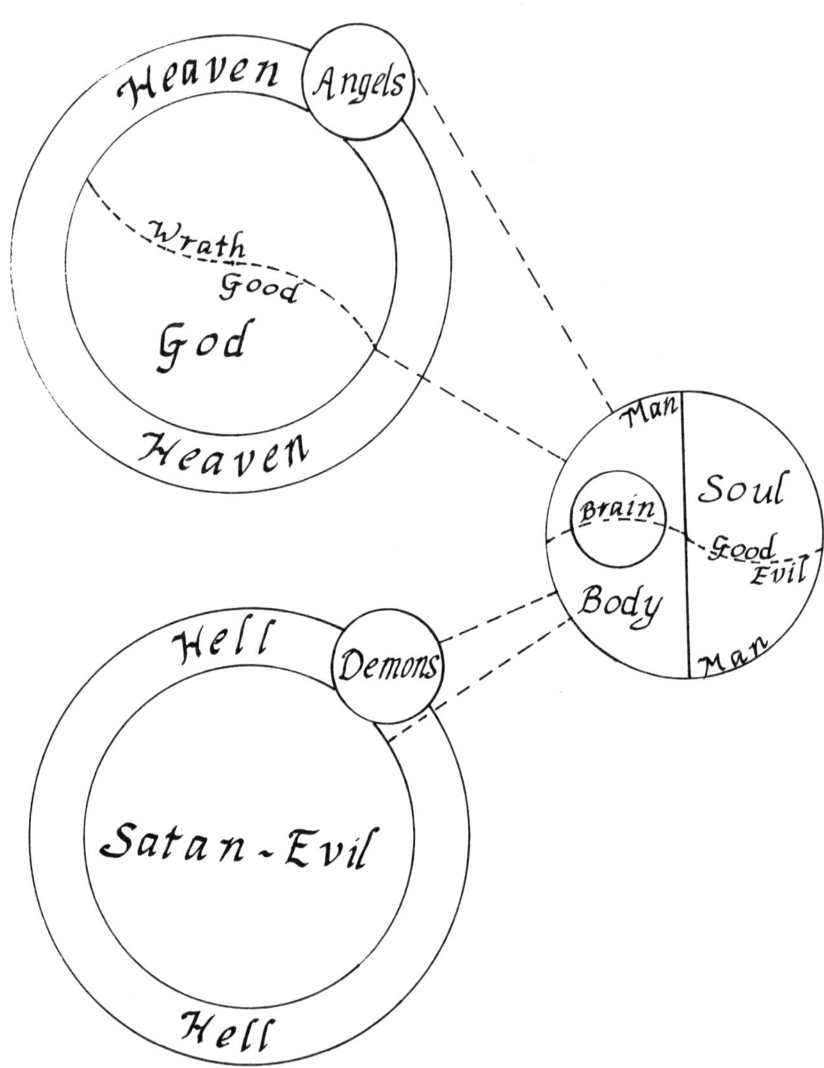

The Judaistic conceptualization of the "scheme of things".

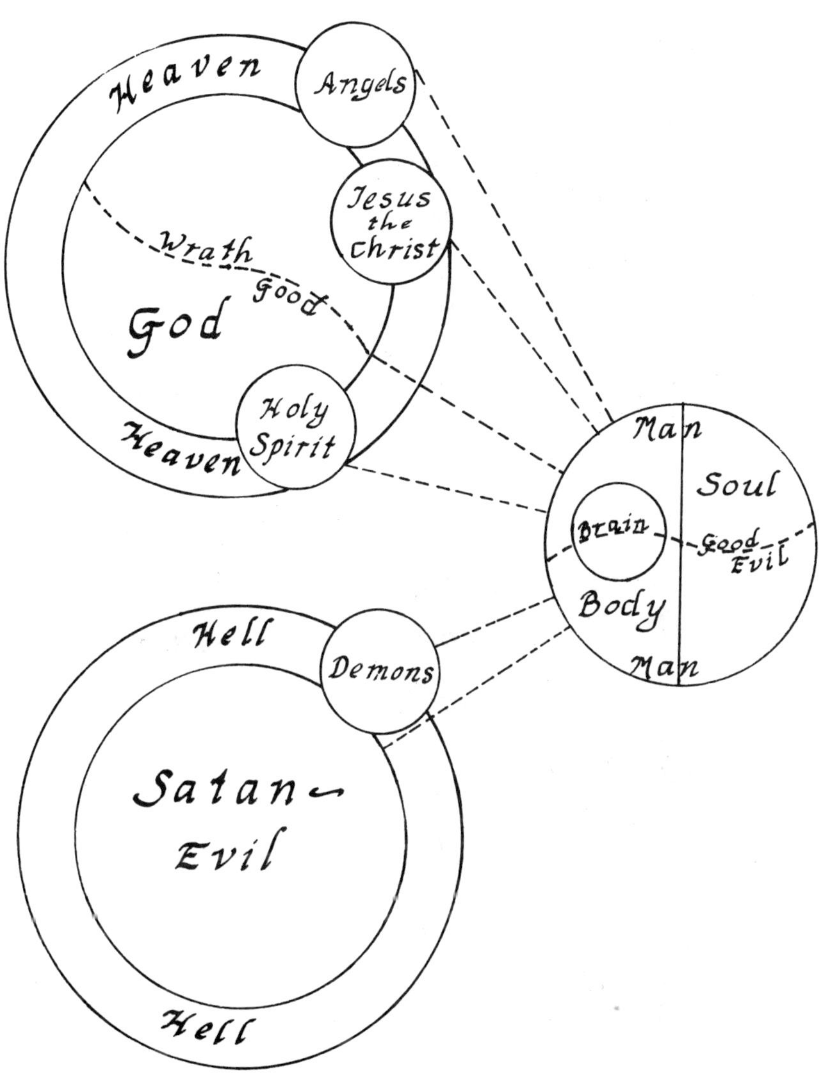

The basic Christian conceptualization of the "scheme of things".

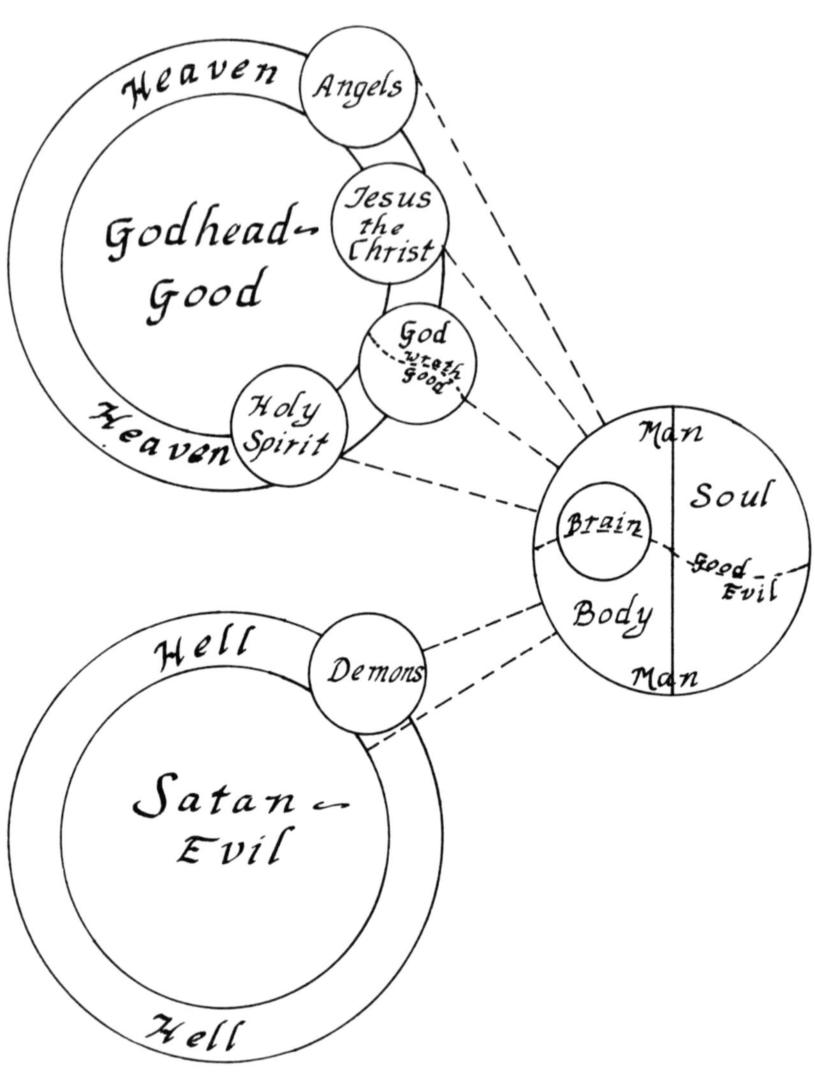

The Christian Trinitarian concept of the "scheme of things".

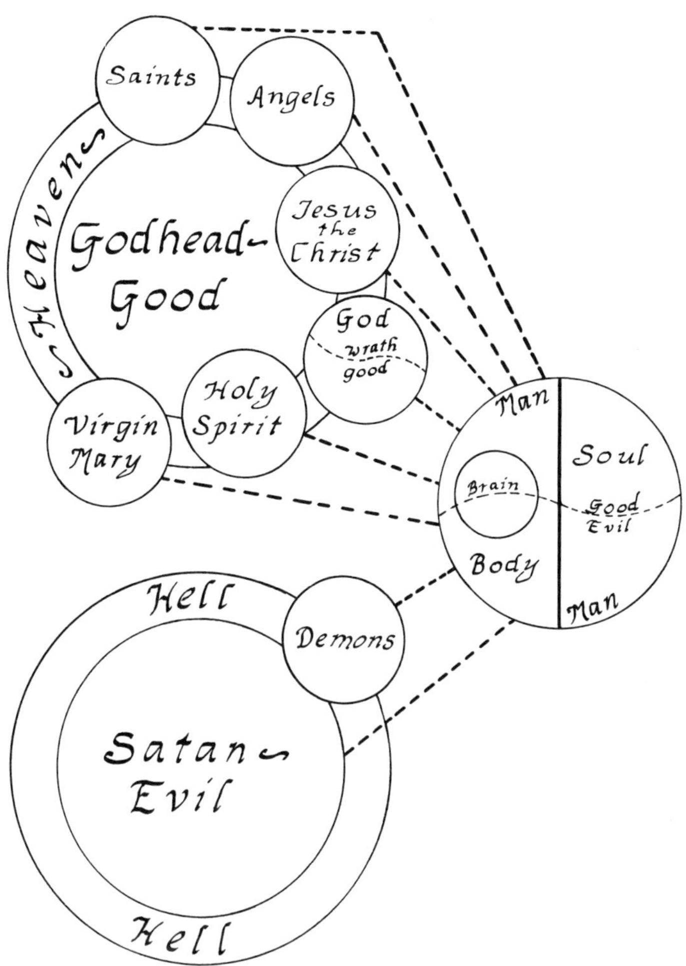

The Christian Catholic concept of the "scheme of things".

It's unfortunate that these seemingly innocent, theological ideals are allowed to remain as a part of our beliefs because they cloud our understanding of how we are of God. It might be asked, then: "Why are they still included in today's religious teachings"? In part, the answer to this question is, that they are logical. They're logical because they are opposites, and man must have his opposites. Man has reasoned that since there is a hot and a cold; since there is a good and an evil; since there is a yin and a yang; since there is a light and a dark; since there is a front and a back; since there is a man and a woman; and so forth; all things, then, must have their opposites. Thus, following along these same lines of logic, it can be seen how it was deduced that—since there is a God, there must also be a Satan; and, since there is a Heaven, there must also be a Hell.

But, there are no opposites to God. And Heaven is not a place; it's the state of God. The state of Heaven is attained when the soul, or the infinite part of the entity, reaches total perfection. As for Satan and Hell, it can only be surmised that they came into being, not only because they fit into the theme of opposites, but also, because of man's fear of the dark and the unknown. In other words, Satan and Hell are mankind's creations, used to explain "why" bad, fearful and hurtful things happen.

The Philosophy of Monodeitism, on the other hand, believes that there is no place called Heaven; there is no place called Hell; there is no entity called Satan. There is no place called Heaven because Heaven is the state of perfection—the state of God. And, since we are already a part of God, we are also moving toward the state of Heaven. Additionally, Satan and Hell cannot exist because they are contradictions to God's perfection. If we acknowledge and agree with the concept that God, in His existence, is a perfect, totalness complete—the Whole; and, if we accept and agree with the idea that the Whole is the sum of its parts, and, that all of its parts make up the Whole—then, the ability for any of those parts to exist outside of, and contrary to, the Whole (ie. Satan and Hell) cannot be. Nothing can exist outside of the Whole because God is a completeness. And too, nothing imperfect can exist within God because He is total perfection.

Mankind must come to grips with the fact that perfection means just exactly that. There is no compromise. There can be nothing more, nor anything less, to absolute perfection, than absolute perfection. Until we accept this fact, we will continue to wallow around in the confusion and illogic that is being recounted and taught to us on a daily basis. Until we accept this fact, our growth toward the state of perfection will be greatly encumbered.

There are several methods of holding someone or something to another. One method is by creating and maintaining an atmosphere of love. Another method is by causing and nurturing the need to hate. Still another method is to instill and play upon an individual's physical and psychological fears. Contemporary religions of today use a combination of both, the creation of an atmosphere of love, and, the maintaining of psychological fear in order to bind an individual to their respective, theological doctrines. They hold their congregations to their theological doctrines by subscribing to a God of love on the one hand, and to a God of just wrath on the other; *plus,* by fostering, within their parishioners, a belief in things to be afraid of, such as: Hell, demons, Satan and, the worst of all punishments, an eternal afterlife without God.

This, then, is the other part of the reason "why" opposites to God are taught, encouraged and, virtually, mandated as a part of a religious indoctrination. Not only do they attempt to explain "why" bad, hurtful and fearful things happen to us, but they also sustain an internalized dependency upon the religion, in order to mollify the fear that the religion had instilled in the first place.

Teaching mankind to fear God—a God of love and good—is a tragic and appalling custom. Not only is it an appalling practice, but it also demeans the beauty of God. Think about what's happening, not just to God, but to mankind as a whole. Think about the confusion and uncertainty each individual must deal with because he or she has been indoctrinated into a "faith", which teaches so many irrational and absurd beliefs. Today's religions dictate that, in order to be, and remain, a member of their specific congregation, the follower must accept, and believe in, without question—

1. A God of imperfection—a God of good, as well as just wrathfulness; and,
2. The need to fear God, who could, in His wrath, punish the nonbeliever by damning his or her immortal soul.

Because one is indoctrinated into these beliefs at a very, early age—the younger the better—one becomes possessed of the fears that are taught. Being possessed of these fears, then, creates a need for, and a dependency upon the religion's theological principles which, in turn, are supposed to placate the inner turmoil and confusion—a turmoil and confusion created by the religion's theological principles. This, then, sets up a vicious and self-perpetuating cycle, wherein one integral part, feeds off another integral part, which feeds off the first integral part, and so forth and so on, until each part is augmenting and sustaining the entirety.

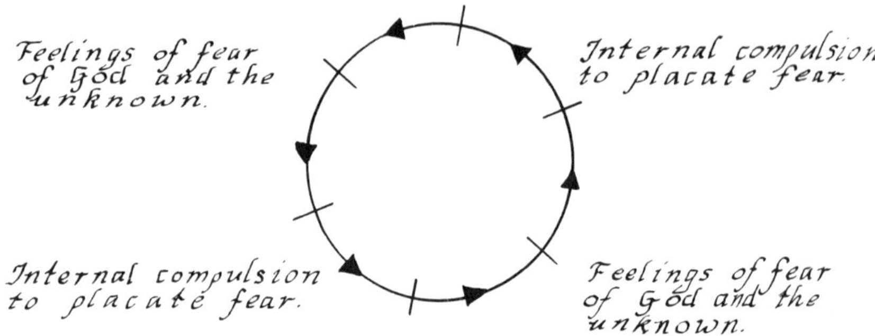

Religion's self-perpetuating, cycle of need (how the compulsion for a specific religious doctrine is instilled and, then, augmented).

In Christianity and Judaism, the fear of God is internalized by way of: threats of eternal damnation; excommunication from the church or synagogue; fear of punishments from Satan; warnings of torments by the Devil's demons; promises that if one isn't found written in the "book of life," one's soul will be cast, forever, into the "lake of fire".

> "And he laid hold of the dragon, that old serpent, which is the Devil, and Satan, and bound him a thousand years,. . . And when the thousand years are expired, Satan will be loosed out of his prison,. . . And the devil that deceived them was cast into the lake of fire and brimstone, where the beast and false prophet are, and shall be tormented day and night for ever and ever. . . . And death and hell were cast into the lake of fire. This is the second death. And whosoever was not found written in the book of life was cast into the lake of fire." (Rev. 20:2; 20:7; 20:10; 20:14; 20:15)[10]

But, it's not just Christianity and Judaism that use this method of creating a need for their doctrines; indeed, *most* religions must, and do utilize similar tactics. For instance, the Amerindian Navajos are taught that if one of their tribe comes into contact with a Chindi, an evil spirit of the dead, he or she must seek out and obtain an object that it has handled. This object, and the individual, must then be presented to a council of Shaman, who call upon the Great Spirit to purge the unfortunate's soul. Failure to acquire a handled object, as well as being cleansed of the demon's evil, results in the Navajo's eventual possession by the Chindi spirit.

Hinduism also harbors its embodiments of fear. Hinduism teaches of the Supreme Lord Kṛṣṇa, the equivalent of the Christian/Judaistic God, and Yamarāja, the equivalent of the Christian/Judaistic Satan. Yamarāja's servants are called the Yamadūtas, who equate to the same thing as Satan's demons. The Yamadūtas snatch, after death, the souls of the sinful, hold them earthbound and force them into their next reincarnation. The next reincarnation is based upon a person's previous life, and how he or she comported themself during that lifetime. The Hindu religion maintains that the soul must reincarnate itself, life after life, because the soul, at some time during its existence, fell from the perfection of the Supreme Lord. The soul must then remain in the cycle of life until it, by relearning the Supreme Lord's perfection, eventually redeems its completeness.

Another example is found in the 6th century B.C., Persian religion of Zoroastrianism. Written in its doctrines is a requirement for its followers, to worship the supreme god, Ahura Mazda. Worship includes assisting Ahura Mazda in his cosmic struggle against the evil spirit, Ahriman, by performing good, earthly deeds.

The opposites to God; the maintaining and the fostering of fear; does one important thing—it creates, in the individual, the need to seek out, and continually return to those who are teaching the religion's theological doctrines—theological doctrines that the individual was inducted into at a very, early age. If the preachers, priests, rabbis, shaman, swamis or whoever, can accomplish this task; if they can establish and maintain a fear, within the individual, for his or her immortal soul; then they can create, in this same person, the need to continually "return to the fold" on an ongoing basis. Returning to the fold on an ongoing basis, in turn, assures the perpetuation, and the prolongation of the need for the religion's theological doctrines, which then, also insures the continuation of the financial and psychological support needed by its leaders. Failure to do so, will, more than likely, result in the religion's falling into obscuration, and possibly, complete dissolution.

The Philosophy of Monodeitism, on the other hand, maintains that:

1. Besides there being no opposites to God;
2. There is, also, absolutely nothing to fear.

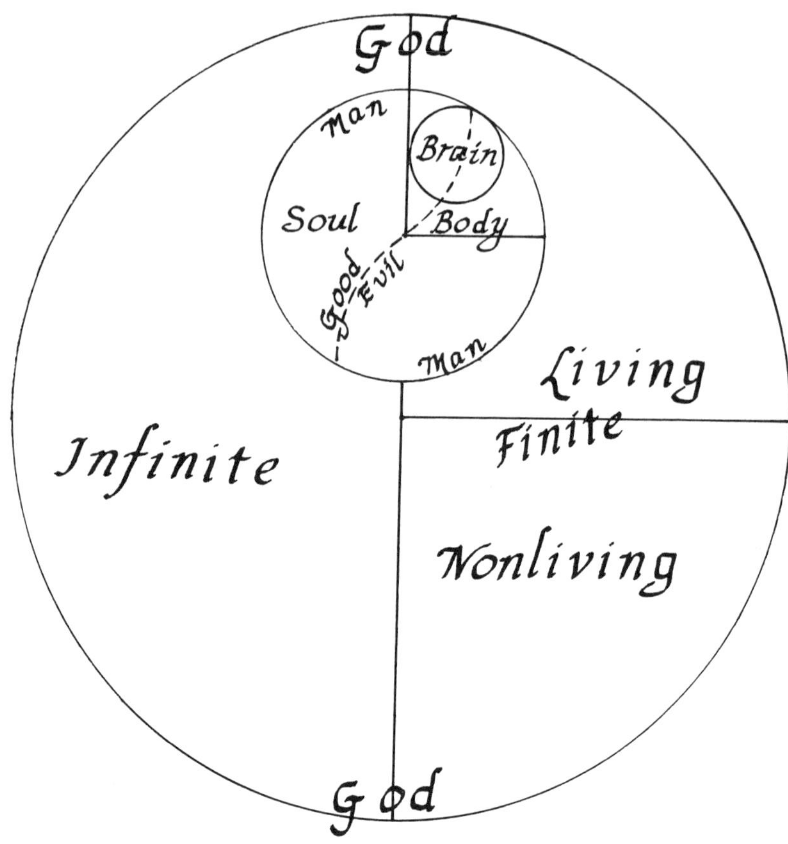

The Philosophy of Mondeitism.

Since there is no Satan, no Hell, no damnation; and, since we are already a part of God's perfection; there is nothing to be afraid of because we can neither be without God, nor outside of Him. We are of Him. He is of us. He hurts not that which He has created because He is a perfect, totalness complete.

The Philosophy of Monodeitism also believes, that once an individual comes to totally know and understand these truths, enlightenment and growth of the soul can again begin anew. It's the fear of God which arrests this essential, growth process—it's the fear of God which must be overcome before we can achieve the goal of perfection.

Part Two

The Realities of Body, Brain, Life and Soul

In duplicity I exist.
        That which is me.
        That which I am.
Because I be two
        twofold reality must be.
                One for the me.
                One for the I am.
Both commingled –
        yet, different.

Of one thing there is a certainty, and this is, that I do exist. Each of us is certain of our existence, but in attempting to describe this feeling to someone else, we become all bound up in the obstacle known as language. In order to define the sensation of being, we must describe the feeling of existence in concrete terms—in those tangible concepts we call words. Essentially, then, this creates an impossibility for us because we are forced into characterizing the ethereal, by explaining it in terms that relate to the physical. Our language, however, does not include enough suitable and/or uniformly interpreted words to accomplish this task. Therefore, we become all bollixed up in trying to communicate our ideas because there are so many different ways in which each of us conceptualizes and/or interprets the meaning(s) behind a specific word; or, there just isn't a word, in our language, which adequately describes what we feel.

An example of just such an enigma, can be found in our use of the word "mind". The word "mind" sometimes refers to the physical brain and the "organized conscious mental events and capabilities in an organism";[11] or, it can refer to the soul, or God, or the Oversoul (depending upon how it's being used) as a "conscious substratum or factor in the universe".[12] Therefore, in defining and describing existence, it becomes essential, in order to communicate, to have like interpretations, such as a similarly perceived definition of the word, "mind". Thus, to effect such a commonality, this part of *A Reason For Being* will set forth, and may redefine, definitions of presently used words, as well as create and develop new terms.

• • • • •

In yours and my existence, there are two energy forces of which we are made. These are the energy force of *life,* and, the energy force of *soul.* Energy force is defined as: "the capacity of acting or being active"[13] thus, "causing motion or change: active power".[14] But, what exactly are the forces of life and soul? No one knows for sure. We do know this, however, they do exist because we know we exist and, too, because they can be seen. The energy force of life can be seen effecting itself in our everyday existence: hair grows, babies develop, flowers bloom and so forth and so on. The force of life has been filmed under high-power microscopes, specifically, in motion pictures dealing with the study of the cell. It is here that one can actually see, via microscopic photography, the existence of life force within the cell. There is constant movement, ongoing change: active power. This, of course, does not define what life force is, it merely illustrates the fact that there is a force present—a cause—and this causality is observable. It can also be seen, that when it isn't there the cell is dead; there is no seething movement, no constant change: no active power within the cell's structure. Thus, instead of trying to define the force of life, which has not been done, we must accept the fact that it exists, because we can see what happens when it's there, and what happens when it isn't there.

Comprehending the above, allows us to then say, that the force called life creates *aliveness*. Aliveness, in turn, creates the capabilities of growth, feeling, feeding and/or reproduction. Within this text, "feeling" is being defined as: *an entity's ability to sense those things that are necessary to sustain its finite existence.* And "feeding" is being defined as: *the ability to convert substances* (ie. proteins, fats and so forth) *into nourishment essential to the entity's growth, sustenance, maintenance or operation thereof.* Life is the physical part of being—the finite part of existence. All living things possess the force called life. The simpler forms of living things have just as much life force as the higher forms. In other words, a living tree and a living man, each possess the same amounts of life force. Each entity is capable of growth, feeding, feeling and reproduction.

So, wherein lies the major difference during life? The major difference lies in the fact that the tree has no brain with which to think, reason and understand. On the other hand, man, being Earth's most advanced life form, does. Man, then, not only grows, feels, feeds and reproduces, but also, thinks, reasons and understands. It's the brain and an entity's nervous system that makes the difference; the brain, the nervous system *and* the brain's mental capabilities, which we call "mind". Thus, mind, in this text, is being exclusively defined as: *the intellect, or, the cognitive powers of the brain by which an entity is capable of understanding: the brain's capabilities.* Man's brain is the most developed of all of the Earth's entities, thereby making his intellectual abilities the most superior. Lower life forms, who also have a brain, have lesser capabilities than man. Yet, even though, overall, mankind possesses the most advanced of all brains, on an individual basis, each brain varies in its ability to think, reason and understand. Consequently, in all living things, the possession of a brain, the nervous system, and the brain's cognitive capabilities, are variable factors, while life force and aliveness are unchangeable, constant factors.

There is a plant called a Sensitive Plant (Mimosa pudica) which, when touched, droops to protect itself. The plant has no brain, but in its existence, it does have life force. Because of the life force, which creates aliveness, it protects itself by collapsing its cell walls when danger threatens its finite existence.

Man, as a possessor of life force, has just as much aliveness as the Sensitive Plant. But, man also possesses the variables of brain, nervous system and mind, with individual mind-capacity varying in each person. To this end, then, we know that a "retarded" person possesses life force, merely because he or she is alive—he or she grows, feels, feeds and can reproduce. However, this same individual may be deemed to have little or no intellect—mind—when compared to a person who is called "normal". This person is then described as "retarded" by virtue of the fact that they are either completely incapable, or not as capable, in the area of intellect, as the individual who is considered "normal". The terms "incapable" or "not as capable" bear no relationship to the terms "alive" or "unalive". "Alive" and "unalive" are words which define life and nonlife respectively, whereas "incapable" or "not as capable" refer to functions that take place because of and during life.

Thus, to have life is to be alive. To be alive is to be capable of growth, feeding, feeling and/or reproduction. When a living entity dies, life and, by definition, aliveness can no longer exist. If life and aliveness are no longer present; growth, feeding, feeling and/or reproduction can no longer take place.

To reduce the concept of life to its lowest common denominator, we must reduce all living things to that of the cell. The cell is the single, smallest entity that can possess life force. The cell has its own structure and is capable of growth, feeding, feeling and/or reproduction. Because each cell is capable of possessing life force, it is also capable of being alive.

The amoeba is a single-celled entity. It's capable of existing in and of its own self. Man, on the other hand, is a multiple-celled entity of which, and for the most part, each living cell is dependent upon the other for its continued existence. A man, then, is a community of cells which all work in conjunction with each other in order to maintain their finite existence. In other words, the red blood cells are needed by the heart muscle cells, to provide food and oxygen to the heart muscle cells, so that, the red blood cells can continue to exist in order to provide food and oxygen—and so forth. It's a closed system of many, many cells, wherein each cell possesses its own life force and, in turn, its own aliveness.

Because of, and in conjunction with the above, the following definitions have been developed:

Body —Body is a cell (or a group of cells) that is the physical part of a living entity.

Brain —Brain is a body cell (or a group of body cells) that is capable of recording, translating, storing and/or reusing electrical impulses which have been produced by other body cells. Not all living entities have a brain.

Mind —Mind is the intellect or the cognitive capabilities of the brain by which an entity is capable of understanding; the brain's capabilities.

Life —Life is that energy force which creates aliveness within the cell, empowering the cell with the ability to exist—to be alive—on the finite plane.

Aliveness —Aliveness creates, in each cell, the capabilities of growth, feeling, feeding and/or reproduction. Aliveness exists when the cell possesses any one, or any combination, of the above four abilities.

Total
Aliveness — Total aliveness is the cell's capabilities of growing, feeding, feeling *and* reproducing.

Thus, it can be concluded that each of us—each man—is a mass of alivenesses; a mass of single entities that are each struggling to remain alive, and in so doing, are keeping the whole alive. This does not explain "why" each of us feels "singleness", because we are not. We are, instead, a whole bunch of separates. So, wherein does the feeling of being a "single separate" come from?

In order to answer this question, we must first come to realize that we are not our bodies—that the body is simply a shell we exist within on the finite level. Consequently, it must then be concluded that there is another energy force which exists outside of, and apart from, the force of life. We, of course, call this force the force of soul. It, like the energy force of life, can be seen effecting itself in our everyday existence: we are each unique in our existence, the tree is a separate singleness, the dog is an individual entity and so forth and so on. The force of soul, too, has been photographed. Specifically, it has been photographed using electrophotography (Kirlian Photography). Below is a picture that appeared in an article written in the *Smithsonian* magazine.

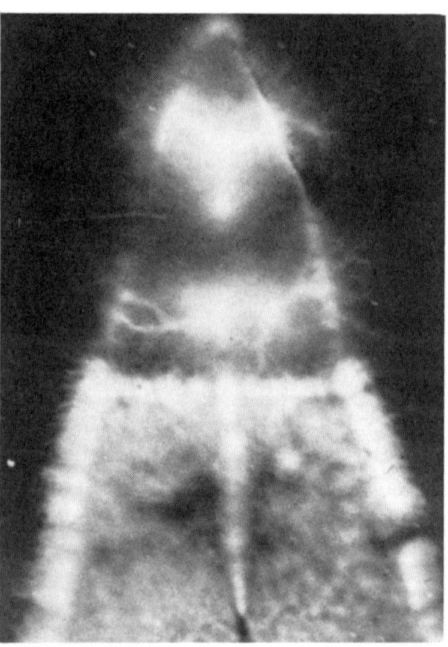

Classic example of phantom-leaf effect: ivy tip had been cut off before leaf was placed on the film.[15]

The above photograph is evidence of what the force of soul (not so named in the magazine article, but instead called "a vital energy") looks like. Although, like the force of life, we cannot define what it is, the picture does illustrate that there is another force present. In the photograph of the cut ivy leaf, the "phantom-leaf effect" exists *after* the leaf was cut, proving that a force, of which we all consist, exists *beyond and outside of the body.*

The magazine article describes a discussion which took place between Drs. David Lord and Richard Petrini, of the Lawrence Livermore Laboratory in California, and Dr. Thelma Moss, of the University of California. In trying to explain what the "phantom-leaf effect" is, Dr. Lord stated: "the reason may have to do with electrostatics." Dr. Petrini continued by saying: "First you put the leaf down on the film, then you cut off the piece. You can't see it with the naked eye, but the excised area already made an impression. It's an ion bombardment effect."[16]

"'No way,' Dr. Thelma Moss retorts. To her, the cut leaf effect is a clear sign of some sort of vital energy at work. 'Why do we get an image when we cut the leaf *before* we put it on the film? I wouldn't see any purpose mucking about in this field if it were an entirely electrical phenomenon.'"[17]

Because it has been substantiated that the force of soul is a separate energy force, the following definitions have been formulated:

Soul — Soul is that energy force which creates amness within the entity, empowering the entity with the capability of existing as a uniqueness—a separate singleness—on the finite level. Soul force is the true essence of each entity—its unique completeness—and fuses with life force, at that point in time, when an entity possesses *total aliveness.*

Amness — Amness creates, in the entity, the capabilities of maturation and unification on the finite level, as well as afeeling on both the finite and infinite levels.

Finite Level — The finite level is that plane of existence wherein we exist (be) during life. It is upon the finite level that soul force fuses with life force to produce an entity with *total aliveness.*

Infinite Level — The infinite level is that plane of existence wherein we exist (be) when we are, exclusively, our soul force. Existence on the infinite level takes place when life force ceases and soul force—an entity's true essence—is released.

Thus, it's the force of soul that creates amness. Amness, in turn, creates, in the entity, the capabilities of ongoing, ever-increasing maturation, as well as unification (its ability to bind itself into a unique completeness) on the finite level. Amness also, on both the finite and the infinite levels, creates the entity's sense of *afeeling;* or, *the entity's ability to sense its separate singleness.*

For the single-celled entity, soul force and amness bind just one life force and aliveness into a uniqueness. But in a man, a multiple-cellular entity, soul force and amness unite thousands of life forces and alivenesses into an entirety. These principles and ideas touch off a multitude of questions, such as:

Are the forces of life and soul, one in the same?

In the scheme of existence, everything points to life force and soul force being two unique forces. This conclusion is arrived at, simply because of this—I am and I know that I am. I am a unique entity. I also know that I am not the shell my soul binds together. I am, instead, my soul force; this is my true essence—my unique completeness. We each, individually, know this as a truth.

Additionally, Kirlian and microscopic photography reveal that there are two separate forces at work. But, as important as these two factors are, it is also the only logical explanation that one, based upon man's present-day, cumulative knowledge, can arrive at, *especially* if we accept the idea that soul force continues on in its existence and reincarnates itself in life after life. This, in turn, leads us to asking and answering the following questions:

Since life force and soul force are separate forces—

a) Where, then, does the force of life exist when there is no living entity; and,

b) Where, then, does the force of soul exist when soul force is not uniting an entity into a unique completeness?

Plus,

c) When does soul force merge itself with life force?

Each of us—each entity—carries the seeds of life force. In man, and many living things, these seeds are called "gametes", or, the ovum (egg) and the sperm. Therefore, it can be reasoned, that since each of us inherits these seeds for the creation of, and the continuation of, the force of life, the force of life, then, exists exclusively on the finite plane. In other words, in all entities it takes life to beget life. The only exception to this rule, it must be surmised, has to be at that moment in time when there was no life force, and all of the necessary elements were brought together in that special "primordial soup" which created the force of life. But again, all of this took place (and, most likely, is still taking place) on the finite level.

The force of soul—an entity's true essence—, on the other hand, exists, during life, on the finite plane and, after death, on the infinite plane. We—each entity—do not carry the seeds of soul force like we carry the seeds of life force. Soul force exists outside of, and separately from, the force of life *and* on two separate planes, depending upon which reality it happens to be in.

This brings us back to our definitions and an explanation of "why" we must incorporate into them, the concept of *total aliveness*. Since no entity, including man, carries the seeds of soul; and, since every entity, including man, carries the seeds of life; there must be a point in time when soul force and life force merge together into a unique completeness. This is that moment in time when an entity, even a single-celled creature, has total aliveness; when an entity is capable of growth, feeding, feeling *and* reproduction. It is at this point that soul force merges with life force. Until that time, life force can and does exist in and of itself for a very short period, but it does so without the force of soul.

To clarify this concept, we must return to the gamete. The gamete (sperm or ovum) is a single cell: "a mature germ cell possessing a haploid chromosome set and capable of initiating the formation of a new individual by fusion with another gamete".[18] As such, the gamete—the seed of life—possesses life force. It also possesses aliveness, but it does not possess total aliveness. It cannot have total aliveness because it is incapable of effecting growth, feeding, feeling *and* reproduction. At best, a gamete can feel, but it cannot grow, feed and reproduce. This, then, makes it a cell which is incapable of total aliveness, and too, incapable of possessing the force of soul. This, also, is the reasoning behind the Philosophy of Monodeitism's axiom number fourteen, which states: *Life has no soul, unless it possesses total aliveness.* The moments before fusion are those instances, in finite existence, when a living thing does not possess soul force. Axiom number fifteen, states: *Soul exists without life;* which defines, of course, that point in time when the entity dies and soul force is released to the infinite plane.

This brings us to the final part of our question, that being:

When does soul force merge itself with life force?

The answer is at the point of conception. For it is at the point of conception when, in most living creatures, the gametes fuse themselves together to create an entity which possesses total aliveness. It is also at the point of conception—the point of fusion—when soul force and life force combine, via the body, to become a unique completeness on the finite level.

Still, not all living entities have gametes. An example of one such creature is the amoeba, which is a single-celled entity that exists in its own singleness. The amoeba possesses life force and soul force. It possesses aliveness and amness, but it does not have, or need, the multiple binding capability that man does, because it is complete in its singleness. Yet, the same principles which apply to an entity that has gametes, and/or the need for multiple cellular, binding properties, also apply to the amoeba. For the amoeba, which continues its species by way of an asexual (fission) reproduction process, soul force merges with life force at that point when it conceives and divides itself into two separate entities. It is at this instant—at the point when each amoeba is capable of growth, feeding, feeling and reproducing itself—that they, also, possess total aliveness.

The time of conception is that moment when, in all living things, the finite plane and the infinite plane unite. And too, the time of death is that moment when life force ceases and soul force is released back to the infinite level.

Brain, mind and a nervous system, in an entity, are the variable factors; life force and aliveness are the constants. The elements of maturation and unification are also variable factors; soul force and amness are constants. Life force, aliveness, soul force and amness, when all combined together, create awareness.

The above principle is simple in its statement, but in reality, is much more complicated than one is first lead to believe. It is so complicated, in fact, that it takes an almost, complete change in thinking about what the terms awareness, conscious and cognizance (including their derivations) really mean. We use these words in so many different contexts, that their interpretations have become confused in and with each other. Sometimes they mean the same thing; sometimes they mean something in and of themselves. Detailed and illustrated in this section, are changes in the definitions of these terms—changes in the way they fit into the scheme of things. Hopefully, these redefinitions, new derivations and new words will foster a better understanding for the terms themselves, their meanings and how they can best be put into a proper context.

The first word, we must deal with, is *awareness.* The definition of awareness must cover a broad spectrum in its description because it's a foundation word from which other ideas and concepts are derived.

Awareness —Awareness is an entity's having or showing a sense (or senses) in existence.

Sense —Sense is a feeling, faculty or function created by, and because of, life force and/or soul force.

If we were to illustrate, pictorially, how, to this point, all of the previously defined concepts and ideas fit together, they would look like this:

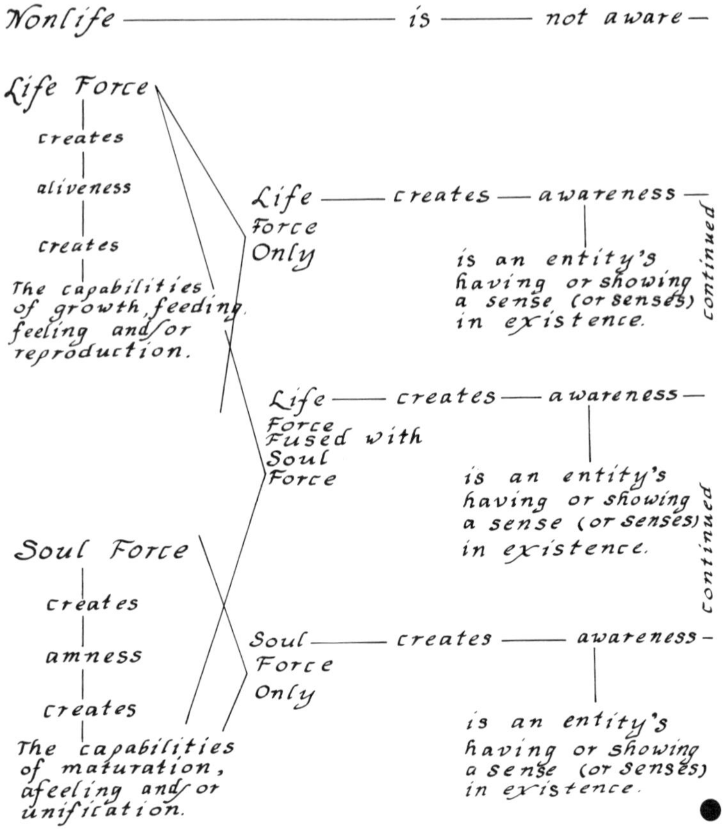

Next, we must take the ideas we now accept regarding the term awareness—an entity's having or showing a sense (or senses) in existence—and further refine them, by redefining and adding the concepts of: conscious, semiconscious and nonconscious.

Conscious —Any entity that is/has soul force, or soul force fused with life force, is conscious. A conscious entity is aware.

Semiconscious —Any entity (ie. a gamete) that is/has no soul force, but does possess life force, is semiconscious. A semiconscious entity is aware.

Nonconscious —All things that are/have no soul force, and do not possess life force, are nonconscious. A nonconscious thing is not aware.

Because of the above, and based upon our total thought processes to this point, we are led to conclude that there are two other elements that can and must be added to these principles. These are the elements of: toticonscious and unconscious.

Toticonscious – Toticonscious describes God. Toticonscious includes all entities that are either semiconscious or conscious; *and,* all things that are nonconscious. Toticonscious includes all entities that are aware and all things that are not aware.

Unconscious – Unconscious is not. To be unconscious is to be nonexistent, which cannot be, if we accept the fact that God is all – a perfect, totalness complete.

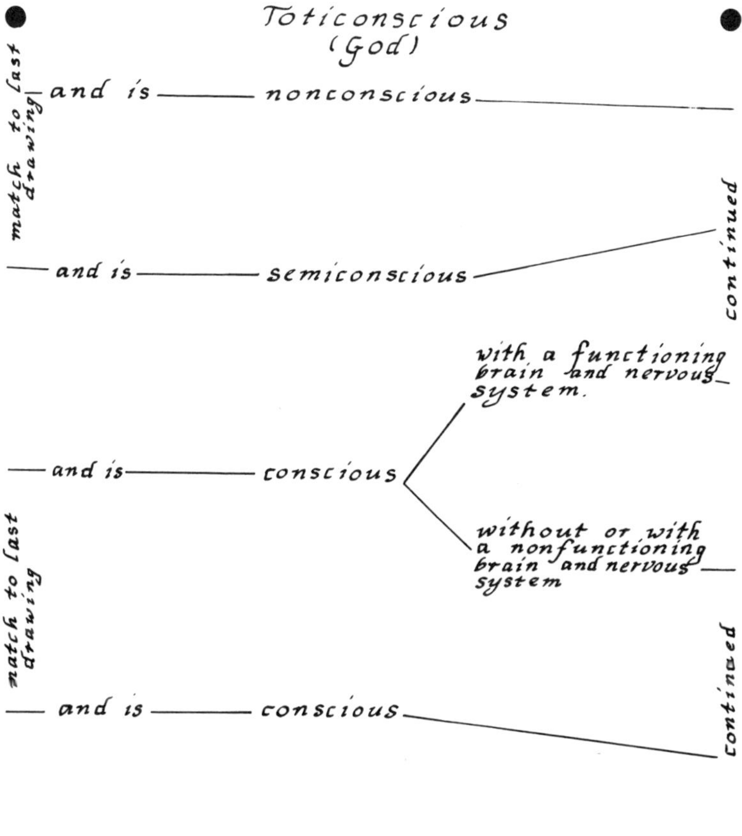

Thus, awareness must be divided into two factors; the factors of conscious and semiconscious. Conscious and semiconscious should not be confused with cognizance or sensation. They are not the same things and, indeed, are factors that are created because of, and from, being conscious or semiconscious. In other words, sensation and/or cognizance cannot exist in an entity that is neither conscious nor semiconscious.

The next piece of the riddle, to be put into its proper place, is the concept of sensation. Currently, only two types of sensation are described and used in our everyday language when, in actuality, there are three. The two types, in common usage, are feeling and paining.

The other type, which has already been partially addressed in *A Reason For Being,* is *afeeling.*

Feeling – Feeling is a primary life function of each cell. Feeling is the cell's ability to sense those things that are necessary to sustain its finite existence. A brain is not needed for the cell to feel. The cell's nucleus is the organelle, within which the functions necessary to maintain its existence (ie. reproduction and protein synthesis) are effected. Feeling causes a cell to react, although the cell does not "understand" why or what makes it react.

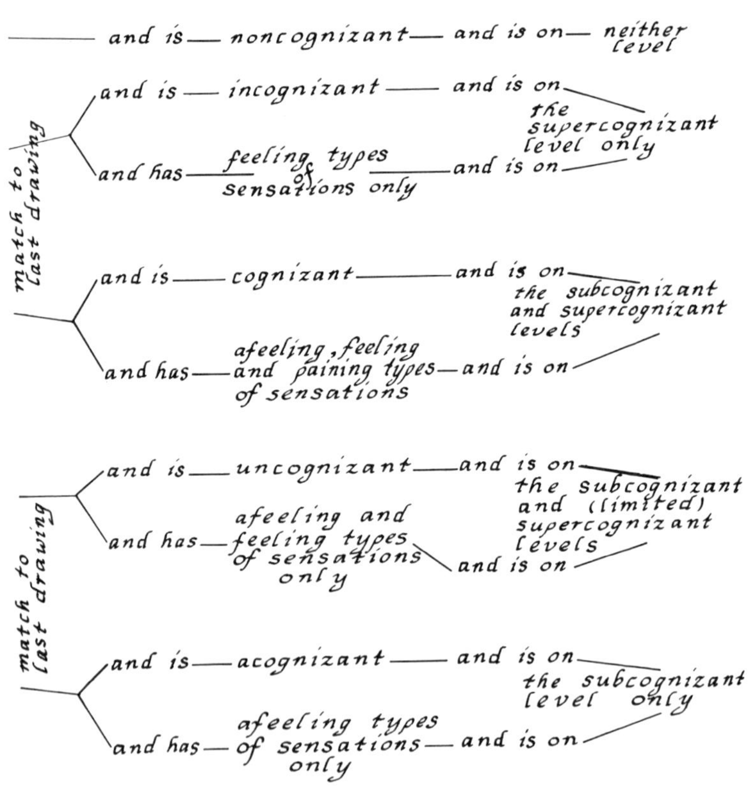

Paining —Paining (not necessarily harmful or physical discomfort) is *not* the same as feeling. Paining results from stimulating a specialized cell—a nerve cell—to the extent that it emits an electrical impulse which is carried along the cell's axon to the brain. The brain translates this impulse and emits its own electrical impulse(s) which, in turn, cause other cells (ie. muscle cells) to react. Paining is synonymous with the "senses"—sight, hearing, smell, taste and/or touch. Paining is dependent upon the brain and a nervous system, for the brain and the nervous system, by way of the mind, provides an "understanding" of why or what is making the entity react.

Afeeling —Afeeling is an entity's ability to sense its existence. Afeeling is a sensation that is apart from the other two types of sensation, in that, it is the entity's sense of all—the sensation of totality. Thus, afeeling cannot cause "paining" or "feeling" which, in turn, precludes it from causing reaction—it just is.

The final portion of the puzzle deals with the ability to amass and assimilate "knowledge". In this text, and to bring the concepts of "knowing" and "knowledge" back into their proper perspective, the word cognizance, and its derivatives, has been used and/or changed to fit this need. Additionally, the above illustration already includes these terms in its finished schematic.

Knowledge —Knowledge is the condition or state of maturation in existence.

Knowing —Knowing is an entity's ability to have or amass knowledge. Knowledge can be given to an entity, such as in the case of the gamete, or, it can be acquired, by way of the sensations of feeling and paining, in an entity that possesses a brain and a nervous system; or, just by feeling, in an entity that possesses no, or a nonfunctioning, brain and nervous system.

Cognizant —An entity that is cognizant is on the finite plane and is capable of knowing and assimilating knowledge. Its ability is acquired from a functioning brain and nervous system, as well as the possession of life force and soul force.

Uncognizant —An entity that is uncognizant is on the finite plane, possesses life force and soul force and is capable of knowing. Its soul force does assimilate knowledge, yet it does so on a very limited basis. Its limitation is the result of a nonfunctioning brain and nervous system, or, the lack of the same.

Incognizant —An entity that is incognizant is on the finite plane and possesses life force only. It has a limited ability for knowing, which is given to it by its host, and is incapable of assimilating further knowledge because it has no brain or nervous system, and, because it possesses no soul force.

Acognizant — An entity that is acognizant is on the infinite plane and possesses soul force only—its true essence. An entity that is acognizant is in a state of suspension wherein, though not losing any of its assimilated knowledge, it is also not able to acquire any, either. Knowledge is acquired only on the finite plane when soul force and life force are fused together.

Noncognizant — A thing that is noncognizant is on the finite plane and possesses no life force or soul force. Nonlife is noncognizant.

Besides there being the above five types of cognizance, these elements can be further broken down into two levels; that of the supercognizant level and that of the subcognizant level.

Supercognizant Level — The supercognizant level is that level in existence, wherein an entity is given and/or amasses knowledge because it is alive. All entities, which possess life force, are on the supercognizant level. In the case of the gamete, knowledge is given to the cell by its host and it carries the same by way of its genetic codes. The gamete does not, and cannot, assimilate further knowledge (until it fuses with another gamete) because it is only semiconscious, has no soul force and does not possess total aliveness.

The supercognizant level is also that level in existence, wherein entities that possess total aliveness, and have a functioning brain and nervous system, amass knowledge through the sensations of feeling and paining; or, for those entities without a, or with no, functioning brain and nervous system, through the sensations of feeling.

Subcognizant Level — The subcognizant level is that level in existence, which *is* the entity's total maturation; acquired from the knowledge amassed and assimilated by the force of soul, during life and from exposure to the supercognizant level.

Using the amoeba, Sensitive Plant and man, as continuing examples, it can be seen that an entity does not have to possess a brain in order to feel. It only needs a body and life.

The Sensitive Plant has no brain or nervous system, therefore, it is classified as uncognizant. In other words, it reacts, but it does not understand "why" it reacts. The Sensitive Plant reacts to the heat from the touch of someone's hand and droops to protect itself.

The amoeba is also capable of feeling. For instance, it is capable of feeling "hunger". The amoeba, too, is an uncognizant entity. When it feels "hunger", it moves itself about searching for things to consume in order to sustain its life. It consumes other things to sustain its existence in order to grow, feed, feel and reproduce. Because of this fact, the amoeba is defined as possessing the sensations of feeling and afeeling, but because it has no brain or nervous system, it cannot sense paining or understand "why" it is reacting.

Mankind is different from the amoeba and the Sensitive Plant in that he does possess a brain and a nervous system. Yet, mankind feels (through each of his cells) hunger and reacts to various other stimuli. The principal difference, however, lies in the fact that he is capable of understanding what he senses—he is capable of understanding why he reacts. His cells feel, as does the cell of the amoeba and the cells of the Sensitive Plant, but its his brain, and its capabilities, that define what his cells (through its nerve cells and paining sensations) are feeling. This ability is accorded to all entities who possess a brain and a nervous system. They are cognizant. It must be remembered, however, that the brain, mind and nervous system vary from entity to entity. These differences are based upon how developed and complex—how evolved—the entity is.

Why, one might ask, is such attention being given to the explaining and the illustrating of this conceptualization of existence? There are many reasons, but one of the primary ones is this—

Today's psychological theories, do not adequately address the issue of, or the reason behind, individual differences. In other words, all of the theories, presented to date, about what learning is; about what an individual is; about what instincts are; about what knowledge is and so forth, do not completely address the questions they seek to answer. The reason they fail to do so is, that they do not take into account the importance and relevance of the force of soul. The reason they fail to take into account the importance and relevance of the force of soul is that the theorists have either failed to recognize its import and existence; or, have disregarded it because they don't know what it is, don't care what it is and/or don't believe it exists.

But, think about it. In my life, I have two sons. Both of them have entirely different personalities. Environment does not completely explain their differences. Genes and physical variances, such as age and body structure, do not completely explain their individualness. There has to be more, and that "more" is the force of soul. The above definitions, redefinitions, rethinking and schematic drawings, detail how all of the pieces fit into a philosophy and a psychological theory which presupposes that all things are a part of the whole, and, that the whole is all of its parts. *Soul is a primary factor.* It's every entity's (possessing total aliveness) true essence—its knowledge; its development; its being—things that are not lost when life force ceases, but continue on in existence.

Another requisite element, that is being incorporated into this philosophy, is the principle of the sequency of the soul; reincarnation, if you will.

Reincarnation of the soul is, of course, not a new idea. It is, or has been, found in many theological philosophies including even, at one time, Christianity. The concept of soul sequency is an essential factor when it comes to explaining "why" each of us is so different from one another. It explains "why" we are certain we exist; "why" life isn't a futile, one-shot deal; and, "why" we must continue to go on living, struggling and enduring the trials and tribulations of life. Indeed, it's interesting to take the religions of Christianity and Hinduism, and then, compare their doctrines on reincarnation, or lack of the same, to that of the Philosophy of Monodeitism.

Christianity, some fifteen hundred years ago, held to and preached a belief in the soul's reincarnation. At least, it did so until the Fifth Ecumenical Council, led, in 553 AD, by the Emperor Justinian, decided to ban it from the religion. *Without* the approval of the Roman Catholic Church's Pope, then Pope Vergilius, reincarnation was outlawed and declared a heretical belief; a concept inappropriate to the Christian faith and its doctrines. Even though Justinian's edict met with immediate disfavor from the Church; it held. And, in fact, its legality is still debated by Catholic scholars of today. Thus, with the elimination of the concept of reincarnation from its theology, the Christian philosophy can be summarized as follows:

> Christianity is a philosophy whose doctrines hold to the theory that man is the only entity who can possess soul; that life is only once; that life is a pass-fail situation—individuals who pass go to Heaven, and, individuals who fail go to Hell; and, that there will be a resurrection of those who have passed—the faithful—with the second coming of the Christ.

Hinduism, on the other hand, has always incorporated the doctrine of reincarnation into its beliefs and can be summarized thusly:

> Hinduism is a philosophy whose doctrines hold to the theory that all life has soul; that the soul, for some errant reason, has fallen from the grace of God; that life is a punishment during which the soul must purify itself, in order to again attain oneness with God; that purification may take many reincarnations to complete this task; and, that there is regressive reincarnation into lower life forms, depending upon how the soul comports itself during a given lifetime.

Monodeitism, by way of comparison, acknowledges and subscribes to the principle of reincarnation. It believes that there is a reason and a purpose for soul sequency, which can be summarized as follows:

> Monodeitism is a philosophy whose doctrines hold to the theory that all entities, possessing total aliveness, have soul; that the soul is already in oneness with God; that the soul has not attained perfection which makes it noncomplete; that life is neither a punishment nor a onetime test; that life is necessary to the soul's attainment of total perfection; that the soul, from its inception, matures and in so maturing, gains the strength to reincarnate itself into higher and higher life forms; and, that reincarnation is not regressive in nature, but instead, is a dynamic, evolutionary process.

It has already been demonstrated that soul force and life force are two separate forces. Life force has been defined as being finite, while soul force has been defined as being infinite. We, as mankind, each possess a soul and a body/brain/life. The body/brain/life and the soul work and exist in conjunction with each other, but each is a totally separate and different part. One exists only on the finite plane, while the other can exist on either the finite or the infinite plane. The best way to clarify the above, is thusly:

First, there is the *that which I am*—the soul.

The infinite part of our beings which is continuous in existence; the part which does not know death; the part which can and does exist on both the finite and the infinite levels of existence.

And second, there is the *that which is me*—the body/brain/life.

The physical part of our beings; the part which can see and be seen, touch and be touched; the part which can only exist on the finite level; the part which lives and dies; the part which provides mobility/reasoning/growth/thoughts while being bound into a completeness by the soul.

For mankind, then, the brain creates cognizance, thinks its thoughts and reacts to paining; life creates aliveness and the sense of existence; the body, because each cell feels, satisfies its needs in order to continue on in life; and, the soul binds all of the parts together so that it can carry on in its quest for perfection.

The quest for perfection is not the same as making decisions about right and wrong, or, those things we have already ascribed to *the pursuit of correctness in existence.* It does not refer to any of the terms that are, or have been, defined as tasks to be performed in the finite portion of our existence. The quest for perfection, instead, describes the soul's goal in existence which is, that it must constantly acquire knowledge (in order to continually develop and grow) so, that it can eventually attain the perfect state. It must be completely understood, however, that the *state of perfec-*

tion can be, and is, attained only through life on the finite plane. This, then, is another part to our reason for being—that of progressing from the noncomplete to the perfect.

Yet, perfection is not easily achieved—it takes time. And too, time is needed for the assimilation of knowledge which, in turn, affects the entity's growth, development and maturation. Time, for the soul, is infinite. Time, for the body, is but a very, brief moment.

To this end, then, the soul will, from the point of its inception, to the point it attains total perfection (the state of Heaven), have had to have grown, matured and developed through many stages. In other words, each

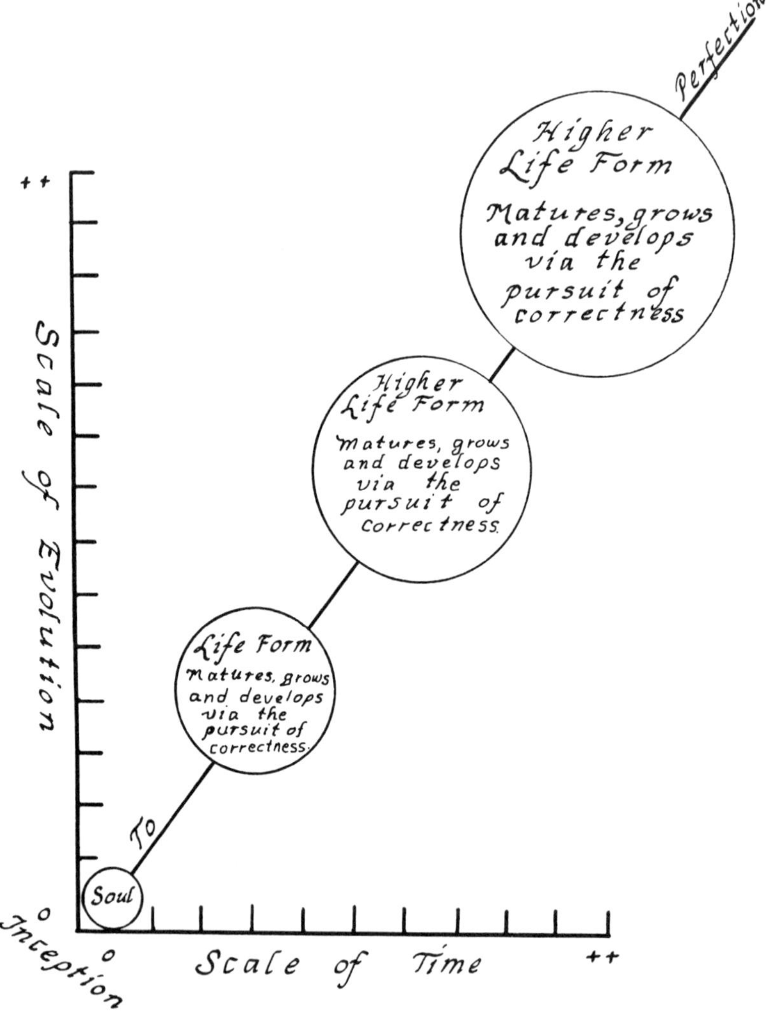

The sequency of the soul.

soul starts its existence with the need to mature and become perfect; a task which cannot be completed in a single lifetime.

Therefore, the only satisfactory explanation, as to how this feat can be accomplished, is, of course, through reincarnation—through the sequency of the soul. It stands to reason that the soul must, in order to achieve its goal, reincarnate itself through many, many lifetimes and into many, many different life forms. This, then, is how the soul matures. It grows and evolves in and because of life. And, as it grows in each life, it also gathers strength.

Strength and maturity, in turn, allow the soul to reincarnate itself into higher and higher life forms. Reincarnation into higher and higher life forms, in turn, permits the soul to gain more maturity which, in turn, increases its strength and overall development. The cycle is perpetual with the soul growing and developing, while it continually seeks, and pushes itself toward, total perfection.

As can be seen in the above illustration, Monodeitism views reincarnation as an ever-increasing, upward, evolutionary process. There is, in this philosophy, no room for the concept of regressive reincarnation; a process which equates to the possibility of backward movement and a belief that life is a punishment. Indeed, the Philosophy of Monodeitism proclaims quite the opposite by decreeing that life is *chosen* by the soul. Life is chosen because this is the only way that the soul can, and will ever, know such things as: colors, beauty, song, art and so forth. And too, it's the only way that the soul can ever reach Heaven.

Hence, the Hinduistic belief, which professes, that the souls of their ancestors are reincarnated into the life forms of Brahman cattle, is fallacious. The soul becomes stronger as it grows, develops and matures. This, in turn, provides an ongoing, upward mobility, which cannot be regressive by virtue of the fact that a specific amount of maturity had already been attained. In other words, as with the body in life, the soul does not, and cannot, *undevelop*.

How long a soul remains at the level of a specific life form, or how much growth, maturity and development it needs to advance it upward from one life form into the next, are unknowns. It can, based upon the above thinking, be surmised that a soul will remain at a specific level to grow, develop and mature for as long as it takes to gain the strength and maturity it needs to move it upward to the next higher plane, whatever that might be.

It must also be concluded that there are life form levels within life form levels. In other words, a soul which has made it to a higher life form, may not have matured enough, during one of its lifetimes, to be able to move itself upward into an even more advanced entity, in its next lifetime. Instead, this particular soul would remain at its present life form level, but because it did acquire more maturity than it had previously had, it would go on to a richer life in its next reincarnation.

The difference between each soul, then, lies in the amount of maturation and strength it has garnered. Thus, in order for a soul to inhabit the advanced life form of a human being, it would have had to have acquired a tremendous amount of maturity by having lived through many, many soul sequences. Only after many reincarnations would it be strong enough, and developed enough, to be able to bind the body/brain/life of a man into an entirety; an evolutionary process which, at the very least, must be a very long and arduous one.

It's also for this same reason that life must be cherished in all entities—both plant and animal—and never wantonly destroyed. It's realized that a man, or a woman, must take the life of many different kinds of creatures in order to sustain his or her existence. There's nothing wrong with this, provided he or she is doing so from need—the need to survive.

Taking the life of any entity, although it does not, and cannot, destroy the soul, does, however, temporarily arrest the soul's growth and development. It could mean that that soul, might have to again reincarnate itself into a similar life form, so it can continue in its ongoing struggle for perfection.

Death due to natural causes is one thing, but death committed by one entity, at the expense of another entity, should always be done with forethought, caution and extreme care. Suicide, or any capricious destruction of a body, is inexcusable and wrong—something that each of us must come to realize, and come to grips with, in our quest for the perfect state.

The final factor, to be incorporated into this part of *A Reason For Being,* is defining the "what" a soul must do to acquire the maturity it needs to effect its upward mobility. This is where *the pursuit of correctness* reenters the picture.

> The *purpose* of the physical part of each entity is to provide it with a shell, so it can exist on the finite level. And too, if the entity possesses a brain, to provide it with the ability to think.
>
> The *responsibility* of the physical part of each entity is to assist and foster the growth, development and maturation of its soul, as well as other souls by way of *the pursuit correctness in existence.*
>
> The *purpose* of the soul is to grow, mature and develop until it attains the state of perfection.
>
> The *responsibility* of the soul is to promote and foster its overall maturation, growth and development by way of *the quest for perfection.*

In the previous section, it was concluded that it is each entity's responsibility, whatever that defined responsibility may be, to pursue correctness in existence. One way that we, as mankind, know we are or are not doing so, is from those occurrences which we can label as *cognitive reassurances* or *cognitive impedances.* Pursuing and achieving correctness on the finite plane, in turn, strengthens the soul so that it can move itself upward into higher and higher life forms. Yet, this does not explain "what" the pursuit of correctness in existence is.

Each entity, as we know it, is encapsulated in a shell which surrounds its being. The shell—the body—is an extremely fragile covering that allows life, as well as the soul, to exist in a hostile environment. The body, depending upon the entity, is flexible within limits, it heals within limits; it feels and moves within limits; but, still in all, it's a very, fragile covering.

Each and every living thing that possesses total aliveness, also possesses its own soul. From the lowly amoeba, to the most stately tree, to the magnificent creature called man, and so forth; each and every, totally alive, entity has its own soul, which is striving for, and trying to attain the state of perfection.

To assume that any living entity cannot, because it does not have a brain, or, because it does not have a soft, pliable body such as ours, possess a soul is a grievous error in analysis. For each totally alive entity is, and all totally alive entities that are, are also parts of both the finite and the infinite.

It is also a gross error in analysis to assume that the pursuit of correctness is the same for all entities. All entities are not on the same level. All entities are not as advanced as man. Therefore, the standards are different.

Because of this, the "what" to acquire maturity remains, for entities other than man, undeterminable; a determination which only God has ascertained. This, then, limits us to defining those elements of correctness that apply only to mankind; elements which can be summed up into three, simple words—*to create good.*

Thus, the responsibility of the physical part of our existence is to create good, which, in turn, matures the soul. The creation of good *is* the pursuit of correctness in existence for mankind.

The act of creating good is a positive role; a process by which one gives of one's self, and one's abilities, to shape a better finite existence for all. The act of creating good is achieved by the giving of one's love, peace, wisdom, goodness, mercy, truth and so forth; or, to put it another way, all of those deeds and acts that are characterized as, and promote, excellence; an excellence which creates a better, more productive life for the self and all entities.

The ideal goal, of course, through the practice of self-giving, and by doing good and creative works, is to fashion and build the best of all worlds. For, stands it not to reason, that it would behoove each and every soul, to make its present world the very best it can be, just on the off-chance it might be reincarnated into a similar life form, on the same plane of existence, it now knows life?

Which brings us back to individual differences. As stated before, environment and genetics are only a part of the total answer to what we are. When we add soul, its maturation and strength, *and* the fact that each soul is in a different stage of development, we can then begin to understand why each of us is so dissimilar from the other. In other words, *the soul is a major factor, that must be taken into consideration, when it comes to comprehending the totality of the individual, or, for that matter, any entity.* Without the inclusion of the factor, soul, our theories on individuality can never be complete.

The maturity of each soul is observable. Its total development, in a man, can be measured by scrutinizing the behavior of the individual; by discerning which people are creating good, and, which are not. The souls that have developed the most, are found in those persons who are giving to, and building a better finite existence. Whereas, the souls that have developed the least, are found in those persons who do nothing but hurt, destroy and harm the life which surrounds them. It's these individuals who, instead of giving, are unable to do so; who, instead of making life better for all, are only capable of taking; who, before they'll be able to reach perfection—before they'll be able to move up to the next higher life form (whatever that might be)—will have to learn to create good.

Part Three

Continuums in Existence

Life is as the river's flow
moving inexorably forward through time.
Each entity
within this ceaseless flow
is of the river
gliding with
or
darting across
the ever-moving mainstream.
Entities who be more advanced
more mature
more evolved
can choose to move with
or
against life's river.
Should against the flow be chosen
unnecessary and distressing undercurrents
shall most assuredly
be encountered.
Each man's flow in life is different
but
the laws within the mainstream
must by need
remain the same.
If one overtly causes eddies
one may find their existence
caught within the calamity
of another's distress.
Each of us must determine
how we shall move through existence.
And then—
should against the mainstream we elect to go
imperative it is that
we do not affect adversely
nor
impede unnecessarily
our forward progress
the forward progress of another
the forward progress of existence.

The Philosophy of Monodeitism is based upon opinion, knowledge and deductive reasoning. In Part One, fifteen axioms were presented from which several conclusions were formulated – formulated, analyzed and fit into the puzzle of existence. One such conclusion, for instance, was that soul force creates amness and life force creates aliveness.

This part of *A Reason For Being* will analyze and detail why it has been determined that the infinite, while existing in its own reality, is a progression of many finites, both paralleling each other and leading to their own goals. It will describe how, by relating the finite to the infinite, there are *continuums in existence,* all, of which, are pointing to a definite and ordered evolutionary process that has an objective and an ending – *near-perfection* for the finite and *total perfection* for the infinite.

* * * * *

The one conceit, that never ceases to amaze me, is mankind's tenaciously, held onto opinion that all existence revolves around him. He insists upon maintaining the blind conviction that there is nothing greater, nor anything closer to God, than mankind; an attitude of superiority that is prevalent throughout history and still influences today's mode of thought. For example –

Galileo, the 16th century Italian physicist and astronomer, was ordered by the Roman Catholic Church, while under the threat of being branded and ostracized as a heretic, to retract his published observations that the Earth revolved around the Sun, instead of the other way around. It seems that Galileo was, while using the newly, invented telescope, studying the Moon and concluded that it was a planet; not, simply, a big light in the sky. He observed and reasoned that the Moon was suspended in space, and was revolving around the Earth. Additionally, he later concluded, based upon further telescopic observations of the Moon and our neighboring planets, that the Earth revolved around the Sun.

These conclusions rocked the very foundations of the Roman Catholic Church, for this was not what was being taught to their people, nor was it what the Church wanted to believe. They demanded an immediate retraction, citing a section in the Bible which stated that the Earth was the center of creation, around which all heavenly bodies must revolve. The Bible stated it. The Church was teaching it. The people wanted to believe it. Therefore, Galileo was wrong.

Galileo succumbed to the pressures and demands that were put upon him, by changing his theories and conclusions to state, that the heavens revolved around the Earth in the same manner as wine, when it's sloshed around in a cup, is pushed up the cup's side.

But, truth causes all things to change. Today, we know just how infinitesimal we are. We know that the Earth is but a tiny speck of dust within the vast expanse of our galaxy. We know that we are on the outside edge of the Milky Way Galaxy and not in its center. And, we know that there are many, many galaxies out beyond ours.

But, does all of this knowledge stop us from thinking that we're the center of everything? Does it hinder us from feeling as though we're the only creatures in God's universe who can think, reason and understand? Does it impede us from believing that only man can possess soul? Certainly, not. So, let's bring our individuality—our sense of supremacy and superiority—back into the proper perspective.

To begin with, we must first come to realize that God's universe is an enormous one and that the likelihood of there being some other life form, on some far, distant planet, is so highly probable, it's almost an absolute certainty. Therefore, holding to and teaching a belief that we, mankind, are something more exclusive, and better, than all other entities in existence, is not only naive, but also a vain, egotistic point of view. Man is not unique. The Earth is not unique. Man is not the only possessor of soul. Man is not the only life form on this Earth. And probably—more than probably—the Earth's life forms are not the only life forms in the universe. In other words, the Earth, and all of its many inhabitants, is not the only "apple of God's eye".

Given the immensity of all that surrounds us, it cannot be any other way. But, this is not to say that we are not important to God, because we are. We are a part of His entirety. The reason we feel as we do—the reason we hold to, and have a hard time surrendering, this sense of superiority—is that the only thing, of which we are absolutely certain, is our own existence. We are important unto ourselves. We are lost in our supremacy because of our feelings of uniqueness, and because the enormity of the finite makes it difficult for us to see anything, but that which surrounds our immediate reality.

Still in all, we have to come to grips with the fact that we are only minute cogs in the great wheel of existence—necessary cogs, but in actuality, no different, and no more special in the overall picture, than any other life form on Earth, or wheresoever. We must also recognize that each of us, as are all finite entities, is progressing along a predestined, evolutionary continuum. We must realize that the finite part of all existence is trying to achieve a near-perfect state before it comes to an end, and that the infinite part, which knows no end, is progressing toward the state of total perfection.

Without going into any great detail about Einsteinian Logic, suffice it to say, that it is believed the universe started when a great "cosmic mass exploded"[19] and began pushing, outward, all of that which it is composed. These blown-up parts formed the solar nebula, the planets, the stars and the galaxies that we know of today. This concept is known as the "Big Bang Theory"; a theory that has been, and is constantly being, proven correct. According to our scientists, the beginning of the universe, as we know it today, dates back to somewhere around ten billion years ago.

"The arithmetic of the geophysicists and astrophysicists is thus in striking agreement with that of the cosmogonists who, basing their calculations on the apparent velocity of the receding galaxies, find that the universe began to expand ten billion years ago. And there are other signs in other areas of science that submit the same reckoning."[20]

But, here's the interesting point. *This whole process is finite; the universe is slowing down in its outward expansion. Total perfection for the finite can never be attained because, someday, it is going to stop.*

"Although it is true that the amount of matter in the universe is perpetually changing, the change appears to be mainly in one direction—toward dissolution. All the phenomena of nature, visible and invisible, within the atom and in outer space, indicate that the substance and energy of the universe are inexorably diffusing, like vapor, through the insatiable void. The sun is slowly burning out, the stars are dying embers, and everywhere in the cosmos, heat is turning to cold, matter is dissolving into radiation, and energy is being dissipated into empty space.

The universe is thus progressing toward an ultimate 'heat-death'; or, as it is technically defined, a condition of '*maximum entropy*'. When the universe reaches this state, some billions of years from now, all the processes of nature will cease. All space will be at the same temperature. No energy can be used because all of it will be uniformly distributed through the cosmos. There will be no light, no life, no warmth—nothing but perpetual and irrevocable stagnation. Time itself will come to an end. . . . in short when the universe has run down, there will be no direction to time—there will be no time. And there is no way of avoiding this destiny. For the fateful principle known as the Second Law of Thermodynamics, which stands today as the principal pillar of classical physics, left intact by the march of science, proclaims that the fundamental processes of nature are irreversible. Nature moves just one way."[21]

This is as it should be with the finite. Our bodies are growing old and will die; the universe is growing old and will stop. The finite is just that—finite; striving for total perfection, but only, ever, able to attain near-perfection.

The whole process is evolutionary and can be mapped out on scales of continuum. From the "Big Bang"—the beginning of time and the universe, *not* the beginning of everything—to our present day existence, the continuum can be drawn, pictorially, to illustrate that we exist as a part of an ongoing, evolutionary progression. Detailed below are five illustrations portraying this progression in evolution. They begin *before* the "Big Bang" and advance, in time, to modern man. Although the graphics are intentionally, as far as total time consumed during a given era, not to scale, and, although the schematics do not include all of the plants or animals ever created on Earth, they do, adequately, illustrate the evolutionary progression of finite existence.

Additionally, each one of the illustrations is designed to be superimposed over the previous illustration, in order to exemplify, continuity in the evolutionary process. Thus, Illustration *B* superimposes itself over Illustration *A* at the points designated as *Planets (including Earth)* and *Earth;* Illustration *C* superimposes itself over Illustration *B* at the points designated, upon both, as *Life Begins;* Illustration *D* superimposes itself over Illustration *C* at the points designated as *Man (Quaternary Period)* and *Man;* and Illustration *E* superimposes itself over Illustration *D* at the points designated as *Homo Sapiens Sapiens (Modern Man)* and *Birth*. Illustrations *C* and *D* have metered gradations which end with question marks. The question marks are placed at these points to indicate the fact that the continuums have not ended; that they are, indeed, an ongoing process; and, that the likelihood of more change is not only possible, but also, imminent.

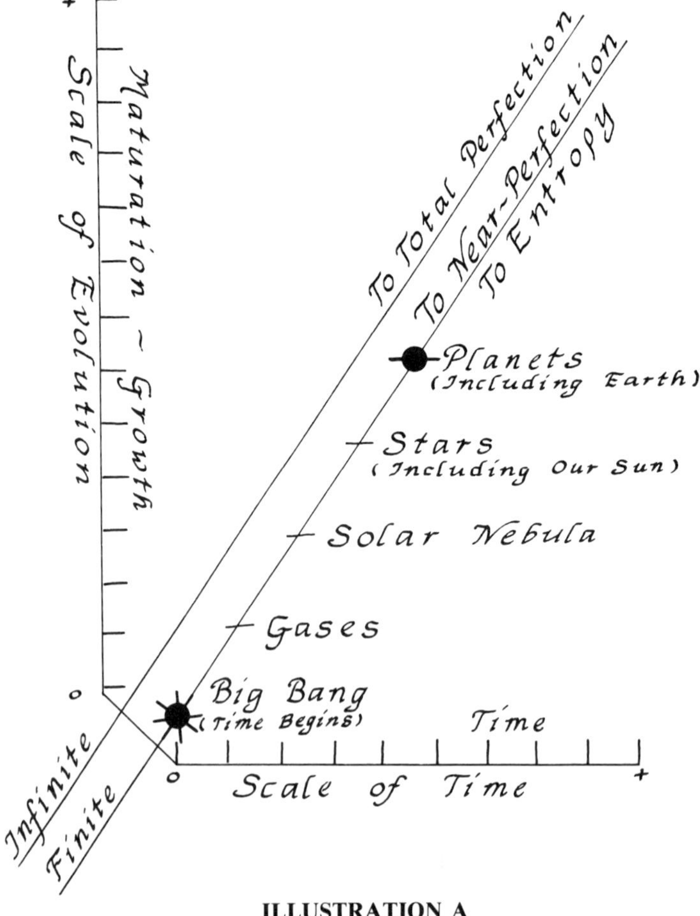

ILLUSTRATION A

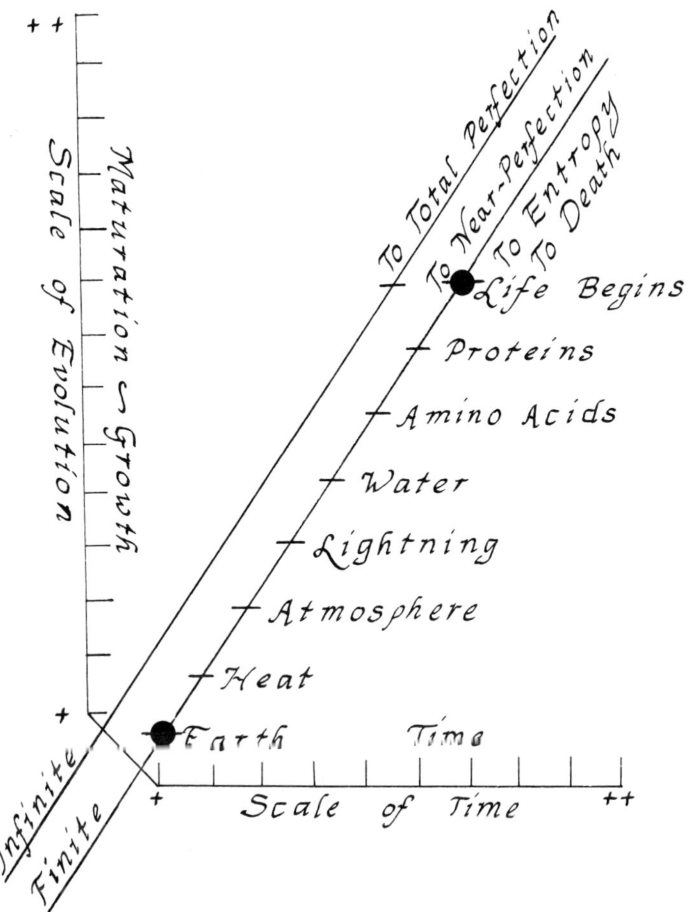

ILLUSTRATION B

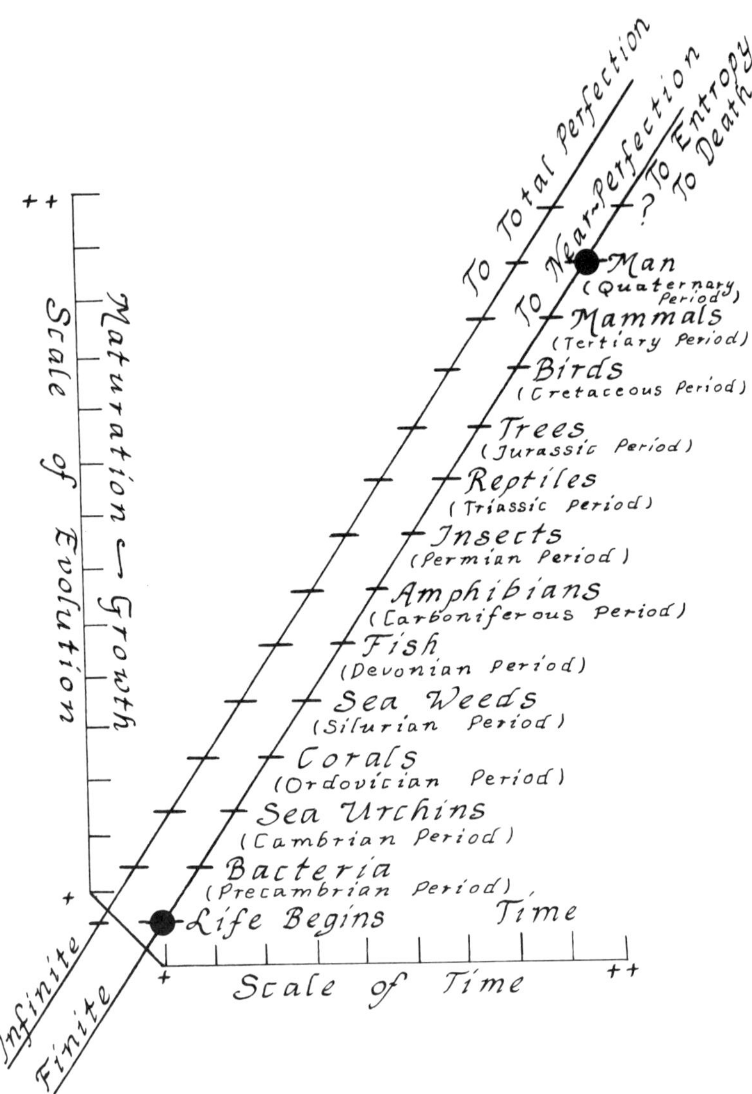

ILLUSTRATION C

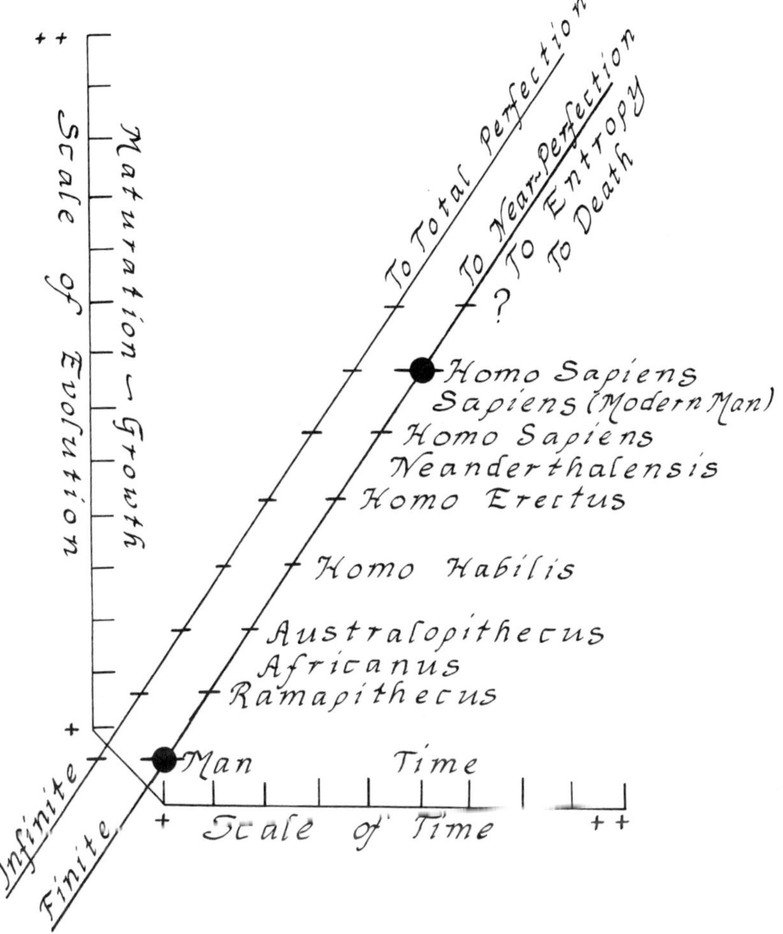

ILLUSTRATION D

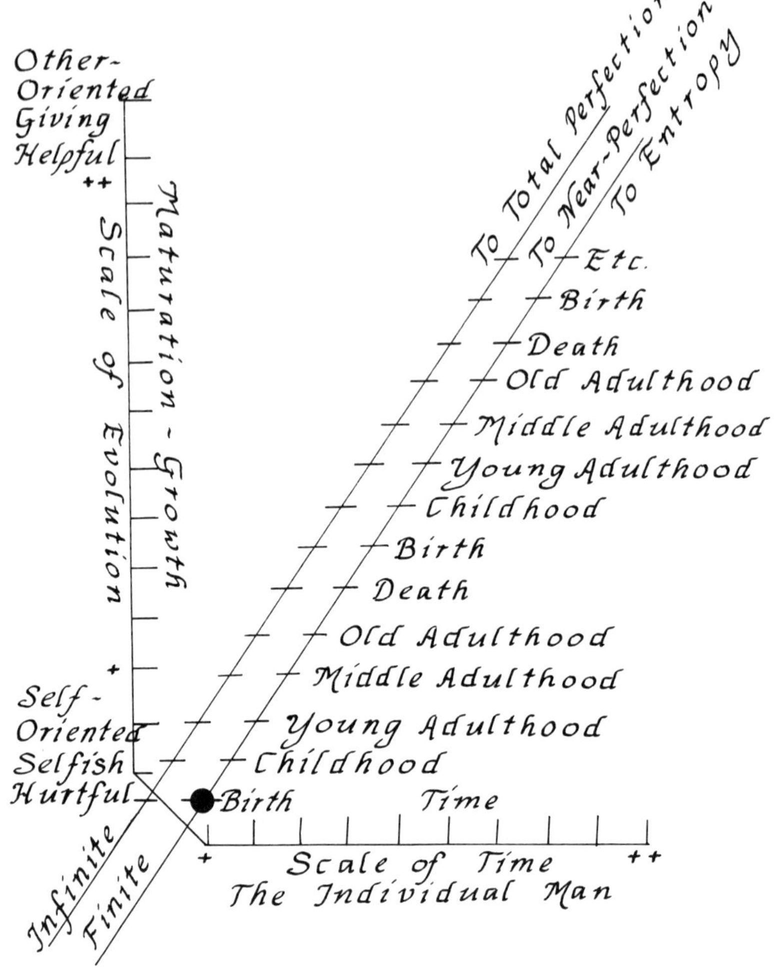

ILLUSTRATION E

Man is not the epitome of evolution, not even on Earth. Nor is Homo sapiens sapiens the final step in man's overall progression. All of our archaelogical, astronomical and scientific discoveries point to ongoing and continuous changes. And, as stated before, it can be presumed that the Earth is not the only planet to harbor "advanced" life.

These same evolutionary principles, also apply to the soul. The next illustration details this ongoing progression as it relates to both evolution in life and the maturation of the soul. In all of the illustrations, it will be noted that the infinite is paralleling the finite. It will also be noted that soul growth does not begin until life begins. The Philosophy of Monodeitism, therefore, advocates the following:

Whereas, the finite did not begin with the explosion of a cosmic mass (this was the beginning of time, life and the universe); the infinite also did not begin with life (this was the beginning of maturation, growth and development).

And –

Whereas, there is an evolutionary progression taking place on the finite level; there is also an evolutionary progression taking place on the infinite level. The finite is evolving to near-perfection; the infinite, to total perfection.

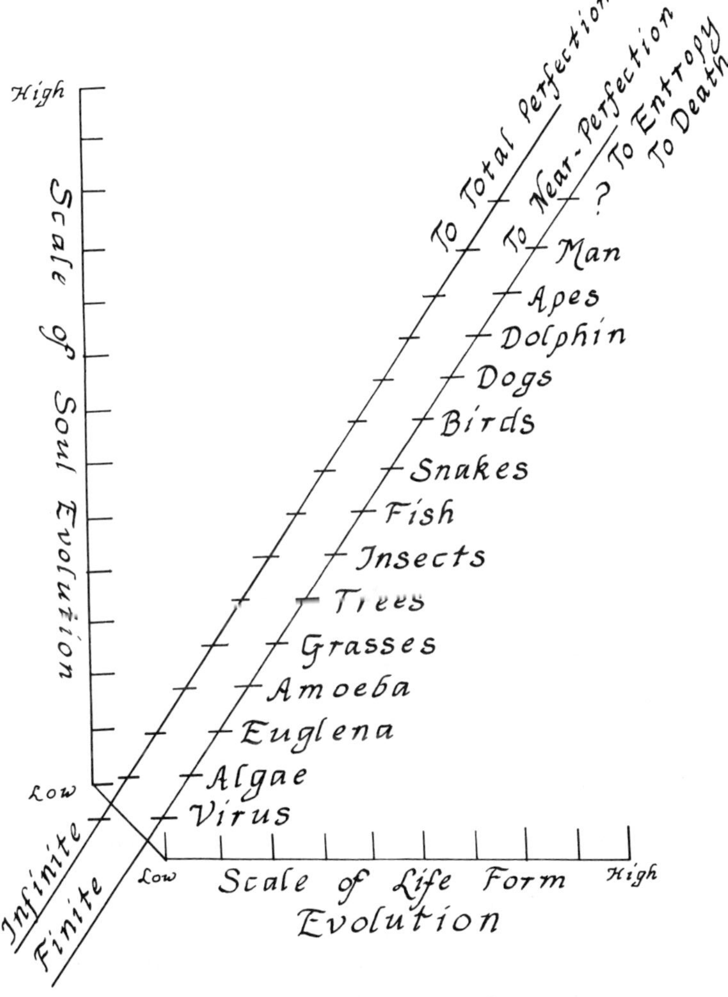

Since the soul is infinite, and is inherent in all entities possessing total aliveness, the only conclusion that can be drawn is, that the soul begins its existence in a weakened state, and then, through successive reincarnations, gathers more and more strength. This, in turn, creates in that soul, the capability of being able to move itself up the evolutionary scale. In other words, there is a hierarchy of order; a hierarchy of order that all life and soul *must* partake in, and follow, to its predestined conclusion.

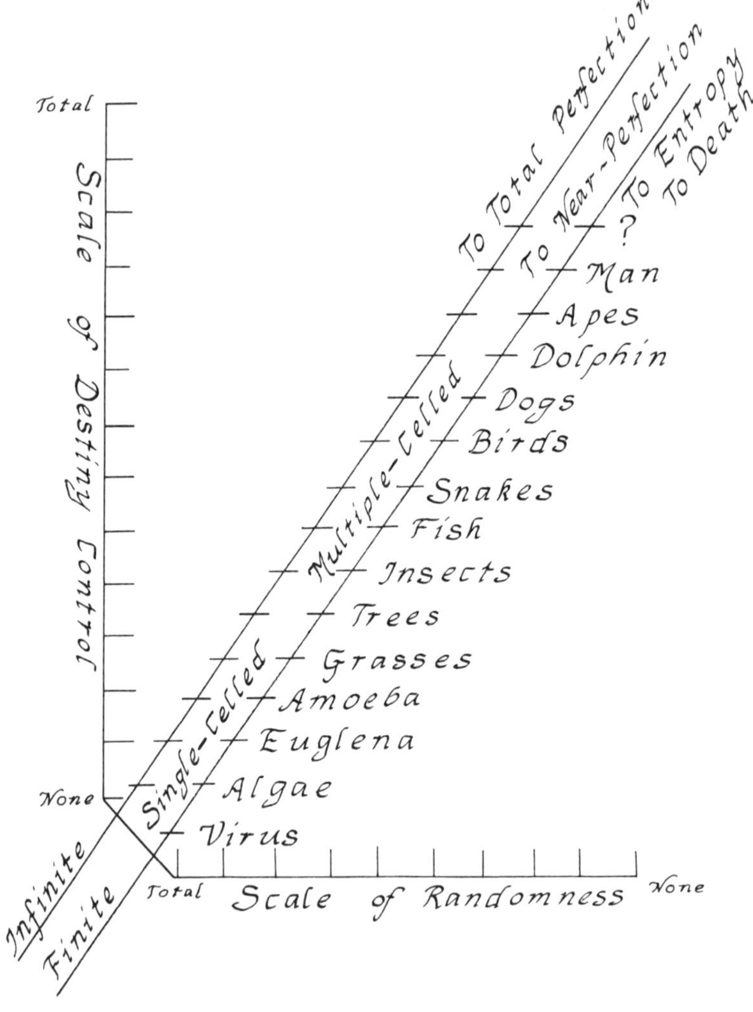

As the soul progresses along this continuum, its capabilities, on the finite level, also move up this same hierarchy of order which, in turn, secures for it, more and more control over its destiny and less and less randomness in and around its life.

A belief in an evolutionary progression, in no way detracts from a belief in God, for it is the way of God; the way of reality; the way of all finite and infinite existence. Our lives are, as all lives are, predicated upon past growth, development and maturation; present growth, development and maturation; and, future growth, development and maturation. Mankind is the most advanced of all of God's Earthly creatures, because he can use, more than any other entity, what he has learned from the past, and project what he knows, plus wants to know, into the future. For knowledge, too, follows along the same evolutionary paths as those depicted in the above illustrations. We are, on this finite plane, what our ancestors have learned and passed on from generation to generation, all the way back to the beginning. All of what we have today; all of the "creature comforts" we now enjoy in our struggle to survive; all of the knowledge that God's smaller, less developed critters have accumulated, in order to assure the ongoing survival and existence of their species; has been passed on by past generations and will have to be passed on to future generations.

Whether or not one accepts, or rejects, the premise that man developed from apes; that apes developed from early mammals; that early mammals developed from amphibians; that amphibians developed from fish; that fish developed from early sea creatures; that early sea creatures developed from single-celled animals; and, that single-celled animals developed from the combining and merging of amino acids, proteins, nucleic acids and fats; is not, absolutely, essential when it comes to understanding and accepting the reality of ongoing evolvement. The evolutionary progression is a fact of existence because we can compare, based upon our knowledge from the not so distant past, what we were; what we are; and, what we are likely to become. There is a hierarchy of order—a hierarchy of order that fits into a master plan—a master plan foreordained and administered by our God. It is God's finite progression; a progression that must eventually come to an end.

And end it shall. For the finite will, billions of years from now, reach entropy. Time will cease; motion will cease; light will cease; and, life, as we know it, will cease. All of the finite—all of its energy—will dissolve and dissipate into empty space. Hopefully, before all of this comes to pass, it will have reached the state of near-perfection.

The infinite—the soul—will continue on until it reaches total perfection. Whether or not this can be accomplished without life, remains unknown. But soul is, and will continue to grow, develop and mature until it reaches the state of Heaven—until it attains completeness. It has been so ordained.

To conclude this philosophy of existence, there is a quote from the book, *Space,* by James A. Michner, which sums up the beauty and awesomeness of existence. It describes, in a nutshell, what this part of *A Reason For Being* has sought to impart.

In the story, a young, future astronaut, John Pope, is being introduced to the magnificence of space by a Norwegian professor named, Karl Anderssen.

"For eleven minutes, while the telescope subtly followed the movement of the distant galaxy through the heavens, John Pope stared at its multiple wonders. And then, he heard again the quiet voice of the Norwegian professor: 'Tonight you've been introduced to two wonders. The beautiful and the stupendous. There are, we judge, one hundred billion other galaxies out there. And if we ever lift a telescope above our atmospheric interruption, I'm sure it will reveal an additional hundred billion. For space is limitless. It goes on forever. Always remember, John, that you and I live on a minor planet attached to a minor star, at the edge of a minor galaxy. We live here briefly, and when we're gone, we're forgotten. And one day the galaxies will be gone, too. *The only morality that makes sense is to do something useful with the brief time we're allotted.*'"[22]

What more really needs to be said, except this—

Be not afraid. Be not afraid of life. Be not afraid of death. And, for your soul's sake, be not afraid of God. Then, once you have accomplished this, during the brief time you have been allotted, do something useful — a something that creates good for all of mankind; for all of existence.

Index

Footnotes

[1]G. and C. Merriam Company, Publisher; *"axiom"; Webster's New Collegiate Dictionary;* (Massachusetts, 1979); p. 79.
[2]Harper and Brothers, Publisher; *"Zephaniah Chapter 3"; The Holy Bible Authorized King James Version;* (New York); p. 858.
[3]Ibid.; *"Ezekiel Chapter 5"; p. 762.*
[4]Ibid.; *"Exodus Chapter 32"; p. 95.*
[5]Ibid.; *"I John Chapter 4";* p. 1120.
[6]Ibid.; *"II Corinthians Chapter 13";* p. 1067.
[7]Ibid.; *"Exodus Chapter 34";* p. 97.
[8]Random House, Inc., Publisher; *"perfection"; American Family and School Dictionary;* (New York, 1954); p. 354.
[9]Ibid.; *"malevolence";* p. 283.
[10]Harper and Brothers, Publisher; *"Revelation Chapter 20"; The Holy Bible Authorized King James Version;* (New York); p. 1138.
[11]G. and C. Merriam Company, Publisher; *"mind"; Webster's New Collegiate Dictionary;* (Massachusetts, 1979); p. 725.
[12]Ibid.; *"mind";* p. 725.
[13]Ibid.; *"energy";* p. 374.
[14]Ibid.; *"force";* p. 444.
[15]Photograph: *The Phantom-Leaf Effect.* Reprinted with permission from *Smithsonian Associates.* Smithsonian Associates, Publisher; *Aura Phenomenon Puzzles Experts* by Edward Edelson; *Smithsonian Magazine;* Volume 8 Number 1; (Washington, D.C., April 1977); p. 113. *Photograph by Robert Wagner.*
[16]Smithsonian Associates, Publisher; *Aura Phenomenon Puzzles Experts* by Edward Edelson; *Smithsonian Magazine;* Volume 8 Number 1; (Washington, D.C., April 1977); p. 111.
[17]Ibid.; *Aura Phenomenon Puzzles Experts* by Edward Edelson; pp. 111 and 112.
[18]G. and C. Merriam Company, Publisher; *"gamete"; Webster's New Collegiate Dictionary;* (Massachusetts, 1979); pp. 467 and 468.
[19]William Morrow and Company, Publisher; *The Universe and Dr. Einstein* by Lincoln Barnett; (New York, May 1979); p. 101.
[20]Ibid.; *The Universe and Dr. Einstein* by Lincoln Barnett; p. 106.
[21]Ibid.; *The Universe and Dr. Einstein* by Lincoln Barnett; pp. 102 and 103.
[22]Random House, Publisher; *Space* by James A. Michener; (New York, November 1983); pp. 64 and 65.